Simplifying Risk
Management

The author provides a comprehensive story that radiates a better understanding of organisational risk, through to the motivations for managing risk and its application in practice. The connectivity of these aspects is profound and enables such an approach to be defensible and more likely to stick in practice.

— Peter Noble, Chief Operating Officer, Newcastle Health Innovation Partners.

With a practitioner approach to risk management, Patrick brings what can be seen as a compliance obligation into ways of working that in my experience have added genuine value to management team business planning and collaboration.

—Matt Margereson, Chief Operating Officer, Hotel Chocolat.

Patrick Roberts 's practical sense backed by sound academic research has gone a long way to embed risk management into many organisational cultures. To the surprise of many this has been achieved without the need for costly software or bureaucratic form filling and the ultimate nightmare of the risk management tail wagging the management dog. This book, for the first time, challenges accepted wisdom on risk management and takes it out of its silo and places it squarely into mainstream management where it truly belongs.

—Mike Stephens, formerly Director of Safety, Security and Resilience, the Medical Research Council.

What is offered is a light bulb moment in collating and translating all the theory into a practical next level Risk Management solution. More than an expert opinion, but an expert solution; integrating risk assessment and mitigation within a structured process. This approach has already added value to the business in dealing with COVID disruptions and associated Global Supply Chain issues.

Risk is mismanaged by most organisations from project selection through to completion. We all know of failed projects which have been buried and careers destroyed; and highly successful projects which rewarded executives but were, in reality, just an extremely lucky punt. Patrick's quantitative approach to risk management allows organisations to assess managers' performance based on the quality of their decision making rather than short-term results.

I have had the pleasure of working closely with Patrick on a number of projects over several years. His professionalism, depth of knowledge and pragmatic approach when communicating the strategic requirements when reviewing a business continuity plan and the various considerations when analysing the impact on the business.

This book clearly explains Patrick's unique approach to risk management, drawing on his years of practical experience in implementing business continuity management and information security management systems for clients. In doing so, it goes well beyond the details of how to do risk management; to explore the fundamental questions of why we are trying to manage risk and how we can measure if we are delivering value for our stakeholders.

This is a must-read book for any CEO or board level executive involved in risk management.

—Dave Watson, Group Head of Property, Facilities Management and Fleet Operations, JLA Group.

A truly engaging, insightful and refreshing examination of the approach to risk management. An invaluable text for academics and practitioners alike to consider risk management techniques differently to bridge the gap between theory and application. Patrick uses his vast experience and extensive research to present a compelling and innovative case, with the focus on simplifying the process and placing return on investment at the heart of the decision-making process, driving efforts to truly manage risk to the benefit of all organisational stakeholders.

—Head of Corporate Security UKI & EMEA, Financial Services.

In this well-timed work, Patrick Roberts uses his extensive practical experience of risk management to offer a pragmatic look at the topic, offering organisations and the groups within these organisations a different and more tangible perspective. It's a refreshing take on the why, the how and (crucially) the return on investment of risk management for leaders and managers at every level within 'everyday', relatable organisations.

—Rupert Johnston, Director, Risk & Resilience Ltd and Specialist Member of the Institute of Risk Management.

Simplifying Risk Management

An Evidence-Based Approach to Creating Value for Stakeholders

Patrick Roberts

A PRODUCTIVITY PRESS BOOK

First published 2022
by Routledge
605 Third Avenue, New York, NY 10158

and by Routledge
2 Park Square, Milton Park, Abingdon, Oxon, OX14 4RN

Routledge is an imprint of the Taylor & Francis Group, an informa business

ISBN: 9781032125626 (hbk)
ISBN: 9781032125619 (pbk)
ISBN: 9781003225157 (ebk)

DOI: 10.4324/9781003225157

Typeset in Garamond
by Deanta Global Publishing Services, Chennai, India

Dedication

This book is dedicated to the memory of
Professor George A F Roberts (1939-2018),
a wonderful father and friend.

Contents

Acknowledgements

I should like to thank all of my clients over the last 15 years for tolerating my constant desire to experiment and innovate: it must have been very trying for them at times. Your feedback over the years has been invaluable in developing the ideas that I set out in this book. In the interests of confidentiality, I don't wish to name any individuals or organisations; but you know who you are.

I can, however, name two individuals who have made very significant contributions to the book. Despite being very busy responding to the Covid-19 pandemic at the time, Joanna Ragsdell very kindly agreed to review the first draft of the manuscript and identified numerous opportunities for improvement. I am most grateful for all the feedback. I should also like to express my profound gratitude to my wife and business partner, Helen Molyneux, without whom this book would never have happened. Not only has Helen encouraged and supported me throughout the process, and kept our business going whilst I have been distracted, but somehow she also found time to review and comment on the first draft.

Finally, I should like to thank the team at Taylor and Francis, Kristine Mednansky and Samantha Dalton, for guiding me through the slightly daunting process of getting a book published for the first time.

About the Author

Patrick Roberts is a director of Cambridge Risk Solutions Ltd, which he founded with Helen Molyneux in 2008. Together, they have delivered risk management consultancy and training to a very wide range of clients, from sole traders to multinational organisations, in the United Kingdom and overseas. Patrick was also a director of British Weightlifting from 2015 to 2019.

In addition to his extensive practical experience in risk management, Patrick has had a number of articles published in various professional journals. He is a Fellow of the Institute of Strategic Risk Management and obtained a PhD in risk and risk management from Nottingham University Business School.

Introduction

This book attempts to place the practice of risk management within organisations into the mainstream of management, looking as much at *why* we seek to manage risk as at *how* we seek to manage risk. In doing this, I aim to bridge the significant gap between the academic and practitioner literatures on risk management.

Specifically, this book seeks to challenge two alarming trends in the practice of risk management:

- The treatment of risk management primarily as a compliance issue within an overall corporate governance narrative; and
- The very widespread use of qualitative risk assessment tools which have absolutely no proven effectiveness.

Taken together, these trends have resulted in much attention being devoted to developing formalised systems for identifying and analysing risks, and the production of many detailed risk registers. However, there is very little evidence that any of this is driving practical, cost-effective efforts to actually manage risk for the benefit of organisations' stakeholders. There often appears to be a preoccupation with the risks themselves, rather than a positive focus on the actions that can (and should) be taken to benefit various stakeholder

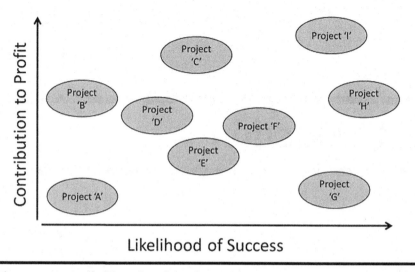

Figure 0.1   A Likelihood and Profit Matrix

groups. This is dramatically illustrated by the fact that a pandemic was the highest rated risk on the *UK National Risk Register** for many years prior to 2020; but capturing it as such neither prevented multiple variants of Covid-19 reaching the UK nor led to robust preparations to deal with the consequences when they did.

It is quite inconceivable that potential R&D projects would be presented to senior management for approval in the form shown in Figure 0.1. Clearly, on the information given, Project "I" is more attractive than Project "A"; but is Project "D" more attractive than Project "E"? How much more would one be prepared to pay to pursue Project "F" than Project "E"? This whole line of argument may seem deliberately obtuse; but this is exactly how risks are generally presented. Even if some scales were added to the axes, descriptive or numerical, one is still not equipped to answer the questions posed with any

---

* Previous editions of the UK National Risk Register have now been withdrawn, but the 2020 version is available at https://www.gov.uk/government/publications /national-risk-register-2020.

certainty. It is argued throughout this book that decisions on risk management should be treated in exactly the same way as any other organisational decisions: on the basis of demonstrating a sufficient return on investment (financial or otherwise). Generally, this return on investment arises because the proposed risk management activities improve expected outcomes, reduce the likelihood of a catastrophic outcome and/or reduce the variability in outcomes. In order to make decisions in this way though, one needs to take a more quantitative approach.

If the use of the word "quantitative" at such an early stage in the book has raised any alarm bells, please do not be put off. There are a modest number of numerical and graphical examples throughout the text to illustrate key points, mainly in Chapters 5, 6 and 7; but there is absolutely no requirement to deal with any complex mathematics. Indeed, the efficacy of the approach that is advocated is based on its simplicity – there is no need for complex statistical methods or advanced software packages to implement it. Readers who are interested in the underlying mathematics are directed, where appropriate, to suitable references. If this book cannot be read and understood (perhaps even enjoyed) by anybody with a reasonable grasp of general management, then I have failed in my main objective.

This book is born out of my personal experience (I hesitate to say "journey"). My initial experience of working in various fields of risk management - primarily, physical security, business continuity management and information security management - proved somewhat unsatisfying without any solid basis in theory or empirical evidence. I therefore embarked on doctoral research, where I found much of interest and potential utility, but not in a format that was immediately usable by practitioners. The past few years have involved many small experiments in applying ideas from the academic literature in consulting projects, commercial training and occasional interactions with business school students. This book is the result of those years of experimentation.

Risk in the Context of Organisations

Risk at the individual, national and global level is a topic of continuous debate in the media. As individuals, many of us take an interest, and some actively participate, in ongoing discussions about threats to our health (physical and mental), wealth, privacy and freedom. National governments and the general public are constantly concerned with threats to public health; defence and security issues; and hazards to the economy. Perhaps the greatest growth in risk discourse in recent years has taken place at the transnational and global levels, with pressing concerns about sustainability, climate change, migration and inequality. By contrast, risk in the context of the organisations that provide us with the goods that we need (or want), deliver vital public services and create jobs and wealth is seldom discussed except in the wake of a high-profile corporate collapse or scandal. It is not even clear what is meant by risk in this context. At the individual level, risk primarily concerns the likelihood of specific events (e.g. illness, injury, death, unemployment, homelessness): does this have any meaningful analogy for corporations and public sector bodies? I will attempt to resolve the confusion around risk in the context of organisations by viewing risk from the perspective of an organisation's various stakeholder groups.

Trends in Risk Management

Writing this in the midst of the Covid-19 pandemic, risk management is undeniably very topical. But this current (and possibly transitory) interest is overlaid on a well-established ongoing trend towards an expectation of formal risk management in all areas of life, particularly in respect of companies and public sector organisations. As Power et al. (2009, p.304) put it, "The period since 1995 has seen an explosion of efforts to codify and formalise principles of risk management ... organizations must apply rational standards of knowledge and frame what they do in these terms to maintain legitimacy". This is perhaps best illustrated by the vast number of standards and guidance documents that have been published in recent years. These include:

■ General guidance and good practice documents such as *ISO 31000: Risk Management - Guidance and Best Practice* (ISO, 2009, 2018) and *Enterprise Risk Management* (COSO, 2004);
■ Certifiable management system standards for specific aspects of risk management such as *ISO 27001: Information Technology – Security Techniques – Information Security Management Systems – Requirements (ISO 2005, 2013, 2018)* and *ISO 22301: Security and Resilience – Preparedness and Continuity Management Systems – Requirements* (ISO 2012, 2019); and
■ Industry-specific regulations such as *Basel III: A Global Regulatory Framework for more Resilient Banks and Banking Systems – Revised Version* (BIS, 2011) and *Directive 2009/138/EC of the European Parliament and of the Council of 25 November 2009 on the taking-up and pursuit of the business of Insurance and Reinsurance (Solvency II).*

In many jurisdictions, some evidence of risk management is also now required by law. For instance, in the United Kingdom, the *Companies Act 2006 (Strategic Report and Directors' Report) Regulations 2013* includes a requirement (para 414A) for the Strategic Report to include "a description of the principal risks and uncertainties facing the company".

This proliferation in official documentation has been accompanied by equally spectacular growth in the specialised organisations representing different groups of risk management professionals. These include the *Institute of Risk Management*, the *Business Continuity Institute*, the *Disaster Recovery Institute*, the *Business Continuity Management Institute*, the *Institute of Operational Risk* and the *Institute of Strategic Risk Management*. Each of these organisations separately produces guidance, and most provide training, promoting their particular perspective on risk management.

Bridging the Gap between Academics and Practitioners

A prime focus of this book is to bridge the gap between academics and practitioners in risk management, in order to place the practice of risk management on more robust foundations. It is a general criticism of business schools that they are too divorced from the practice of management: there is not the level of interaction between academics and practitioners (of management) that you would expect to see in, for example, medical schools or engineering departments. This criticism seems to be particularly apt in the case of risk management. Academic research into risk management is dispersed across multiple business disciplines, including economics/finance, strategy, organisational behaviour and operations management; so there is not even a single academic discourse for practising managers to try to engage with. I will attempt to pull together some of these disparate strands, drawing on the most appropriate theories and research to support the proposed approach to risk management.

In attempting to achieve constructive interaction between academia and practice, it is important to acknowledge that, sadly, the vast majority of academic research on risk management within organisations has historically been based on studies of large, US-based corporations. There has been comparatively little research on firms based outside the United States, and research on small and medium-sized enterprises, not-for-profit and public sector organisations is very limited indeed. Nevertheless, I will argue that many of the principles derived from research on large, US-based corporations are still applicable to other types of organisations, although their application may require some careful thought.

Meanwhile, as noted above, the risk management profession has fragmented into many different sub-professions as practice has developed at a pace over recent years. One of the most prominent sub-groups focuses on compliance with regulations, "good practice" and formal management systems, even where there is no theoretical or evidence base for the efficacy of these. Yet another sub-group is purely focused on managing operational risk within the financial services sector, and has developed very sophisticated mathematical, data-driven approaches to quantifying these specific risks. Looking more broadly, people who would regard themselves as "risk management professionals" are only the very tip of the iceberg. The vast majority of practical risk management is carried out by people such as health and safety managers, emergency planners, physical security managers, information security managers, supply chain specialists and facilities managers. It is hoped that by presenting risk management decisions as straightforward questions of return on investment, the proposed approach is accessible to these many and various professional disciplines.

Terminology, References and Structure

In attempting to take the risk management debate to the widest possible audience, embracing the vital public and not-for-profit sectors, it is necessary to say a few words about terminology. Throughout the book the term "corporate" is used to refer to the highest level of decision-making within a legal entity, whether that entity is a corporation or any other type of organisation; likewise, "business" is often used as a shorthand for "organisational". Continuing in this vein, the term "customers" is intended to also embrace "members" and "service users" as appropriate; and "staff" is intended to include "volunteers". The term "outcome" is generally used instead of a more specific term such as "profit", unless referring to a particular empirical study or a discussion specific to the private sector. Whilst these outcomes are generally expressed in financial terms, that need not be the case: in public and not-for-profit organisations, non-financial metrics (such as levels of activity) may be more appropriate.

Specific references are listed in the chapters in which they occur, but I should like to highlight two works that very much underpin the whole of the book. *"A Behavioral Theory of the Firm"* (Cyert and March (1992)) explores how decisions *are really made* in large organisations (as opposed to the numerous normative models of how decisions *should* be made in an economically rational manner). Many of the findings from this detailed study of the workings of complex modern organisations inform the discussions which follow on how to approach risk management. The second foundation of the current book is *"The Failure of Risk Management: Why it's Broken and How to Fix It"* (Hubbard (2020)). Although the first edition was published over ten years ago, its observations on the widespread flaws in the implementation of risk management are, sadly, as valid today as they were then. In keeping with the pragmatic approach outlined above, I have tried to limit references to academic articles to the absolute minimum, but it is necessary to include some important ones in order to allow the interested reader to follow up in more detail.

The rest of the book is structured as follows. Chapter 1 goes back to basics to explore the question of what is meant by "risk" in the context of organisations? Laying the foundation for the rest of the book, it is argued that risk must be considered from the point of view of each of the organisation's various stakeholder groups. Chapter 2 then looks at the various reasons why these different stakeholder groups may wish to try to manage risk. The next four chapters then look at how we seek to manage risk. Chapter 3 introduces the concept of integrated risk management and critiques one specific approach, as described in ISO 31000, highlighting where the proposed approach deviates from this guidance. Chapters 4, 5 and 6 then explain in detail the practical approach to risk management at the heart of this book. Chapter 7 considers the much-neglected topic of how to measure the effectiveness of risk management, from the impact of individual risk mitigation interventions through to the value created by complete risk management programmes. Chapter 8 concludes the book by exploring some themes that underpin the discussions in previous chapters, such as the relationship between risk management and strategy, and summarises the key ideas from previous chapters.

The material in the main body of the book is complemented by four annexes:

- Annex A summarises a study of the relationship between accounting measures of risk and performance in large UK firms;
- Annex B describes a study to investigate how large UK firms that have adopted good practice in risk management performed relative to their peers during the Covid-19 pandemic;
- Annex C is an illustrative example of quantitative risk management being applied in a public sector/not-for-profit context; and
- Annex D provides some useful sources of risk information.

References

Cyert and March, 1992, *A Behavioral Theory of the Firm*, 2nd Edition, Malden, MA: Blackwell.

Hubbard D, 2020, *The Failure of Risk Management: Why it's Broken and How to Fix It*, 2nd Edition, Hoboken, NJ: Wiley.

Power M, Scheytt T, Soin K and Sahlin K, 2009, Reputational Risk as a Logic of Organizing in Late Modernity, *Organization Studies*, 30(2/3): 301–324.

List of Figures and Tables

Figures

Tables

Testimonials

"The author provides a comprehensive story that radiates a better understanding of organisational risk, through to the motivations for managing risk and its application in practice. The connectivity of these aspects is profound and enables such an approach to be defensible and more likely to stick in practice".

Peter Noble, Chief Operating Officer, Newcastle Health Innovation Partners.

"With a practitioner approach to risk management, Patrick brings what can be seen as a compliance obligation into ways of working that in my experience have added genuine value to management team business planning and collaboration".

Matt Margereson, Chief Operating Officer, Hotel Chocolat.

"Patrick Roberts 's practical sense backed by sound academic research has gone a long way to embed risk management into many organisational cultures. To the surprise of many this has been achieved without the need for costly software or bureaucratic form filling and the ultimate nightmare of the risk management tail wagging the management dog. This book, for the first time, challenges accepted wisdom on risk

management and takes it out of its silo and places it squarely into mainstream management where it truly belongs".

Mike Stephens, formerly Director of Safety, Security and Resilience, the Medical Research Council.

"What is offered is a light bulb moment in collating and translating all the theory into a practical next level Risk Management solution. More than an expert opinion, but an expert solution; integrating risk assessment and mitigation within a structured process. This approach has already added value to the business in dealing with COVID disruptions and associated Global Supply Chain issues".

Malcolm Watling, Group Sourcing Director, Domino Printing Sciences.

"Risk is mismanaged by most organisations, from project selection through to completion. We all know of failed projects which have been buried and careers destroyed; and highly successful projects which rewarded executives but were, in reality, just an extremely lucky punt. Patrick's quantitative approach to risk management allows organisations to assess managers' performance based on the quality of their decision making rather than short-term results".

Sean Blackburn fixed failing projects whilst at McKinsey and now growing businesses as an executive within global organisations.

Chapter 1

What Do We Mean by Risk?

This is categorically not an academic text, and this chapter is not a discussion of semantics. But, in order to have a productive discussion of why and how we try to manage risk within organisations (and indeed how we measure the effectiveness of our attempts to do so) in subsequent chapters, some clarity is needed on what is meant by the word.

This chapter begins by looking at some fundamental issues around how risk may be defined. This leads naturally into a discussion of the risk perspectives of different stakeholder groups, focusing particularly on owners, senior managers and lenders. This is followed by a brief discussion of how the tensions that inevitably arise between these different stakeholder groups may be managed. The chapter concludes by briefly reviewing some common risk measures and categorisations of risk that will be of utility in later chapters.

DOI: 10.4324/9781003225157-1

Upside and Downside Risk

In everyday usage, the term "risk" generally has negative connotations - few people talk about the risk of a pay rise or promotion at work, or the risk of their team winning the FA Cup – and many academics and practitioners follow this convention. However, others argue that risk concerns both positive and negative outcomes, e.g. "Risk is defined as uncertainty of outcome, whether positive opportunity or negative threat" (Chittenden (2006, p.9)). In particular, within the finance literature, there is a long history of equating risk with variance in returns, an entirely symmetrical measure of variability in outcomes. As will be discussed in more detail below, in any given situation, different stakeholders may quite legitimately take different views on whether positive outcomes are relevant to their risk perspective.

Risk versus Uncertainty

In academic circles, many writers still refer back to Frank Knight's (1964, p.205) classic distinction between risk and uncertainty, which limits the use of the term "risk" to situations in which the probabilities of each outcome are precisely known. Knight was entirely correct in highlighting that all meaningful business decisions involve an element of uncertainty: running any complex organisation is not a simple game of chance with well-defined rules and perfectly calculable probabilities of different outcomes. However, I would suggest that not applying the term risk to these situations is perverse and goes against common sense usage of language. Moreover, Knight's distinction suggests a clear dichotomy between calculable and non-calculable uncertainties, when the reality is some sort of continuum. The approach taken throughout this book is to always estimate probabilities of events as accurately as possible, accepting that, in any question of real practical interest, there will always be a level of uncertainty. This is no different to any other business decision using forecasts or estimates. As discussed in Chapters 5 and 6, managing risk effectively largely depends on understanding, and reducing as far as possible, the uncertainty in these estimates.

I would propose that the following is a more practically useful distinction between uncertainty and risk, based on the everyday use of language. We experience uncertainty about the future in all areas of life, but many of these gaps in our knowledge have no consequences; risk exists only where uncertainty about the future has potential consequences for us. Following this distinction, I am merely uncertain about the weather tomorrow in Tokyo, but the weather in Manchester presents a significant risk to me (of getting wet, of getting cold or, less likely, suffering from heat exhaustion). This leads to the idea of risk being a combination of the impact and likelihood of some uncertain future event. The concept of risk as a combination of impact and likelihood has sound historical roots, dating back to at least 1662: "Fear of harm ought to be proportional not merely to the gravity of the harm, but also to the probability of the event" (quoted in Bernstein (1996, p. 71)). This sentiment is also codified in all modern good practice guidance, e.g. "Risk is the combination of the probability of an event and its consequences" (ISO (2002, p.2)).

Risk to Whom?

Acceptance that a risk involves some consequence or impact inevitably prompts the question "Risk to whom?" Clearly, in the example above, the weather in Tokyo tomorrow does present a risk to many millions of people, just not to me. The idea of risk to whom is a crucial consideration in any discussion of risk in the context of organisations, where even relatively small organisations have a wide range of stakeholders – owners/shareholders, directors/trustees, staff/volunteers, customers/service users – each of whom may have very different beliefs about the likelihood of various future events and be differentially affected by these events should they occur. It is therefore generally meaningless to talk about risk as a one-dimensional concept. It is interesting to note that March and Shapira (1987, p.1408) found a willing acceptance that risk is multi-dimensional amongst practising managers: "although quantities are used in discussing risk, and managers seek precision in estimating risk, most show little desire to reduce risk to a single quantifiable construct". In particular, it makes no sense to talk about the "risk to the firm" (or other organisation); it is necessary to consider separately the different risks to the various stakeholder groups. I discuss the risk perspectives of some of the key stakeholder groups below.

Much of the academic discussion of organisational risk has focused largely, or even exclusively, on the perspective of owners or shareholders. Clearly, any approach to risk management based only on their perspective will be inherently limited, not least because it has no relevance to the public and not-for-profit sectors. However, where some form of ownership exists, owners represent an important stakeholder group to be considered. I will therefore begin by looking at the risk perspective of owners; this will be followed by a discussion of the risk perspectives of senior managers, lenders, staff and other stakeholders.

Owners

Since the middle of the twentieth century, the finance literature has focused on the variability of returns as the principal risk to owners (usually meaning shareholders). According to Utility Theory (see sidebar), any such variability is undesirable, and investors will require some form of compensation to bear this risk. Markowitz (1952, p.89) never actually equated risk and variance, stating only that: "Usually if the term 'yield' were replaced by ... 'expected return' and 'risk' by 'variance of return', little change of apparent meaning would result". Sadly though, this aspect of his seminal work on investment portfolios has been serially misrepresented in the finance literature, and variance is often taken to be synonymous with risk.

UTILITY THEORY SIDE-BAR

Bernoulli first elaborated Utility Theory, that the usefulness or "utility" of any additional wealth decreases as we get richer, in 1738. This has been expressed mathematically in various different ways over the centuries, but all of these result in a curve with a gradually decreasing gradient such as that illustrated in Figure 1.1.

The application of the theory to uncertain outcomes is relatively straightforward, as illustrated in the graph. The solid line represents a certain amount of wealth and its

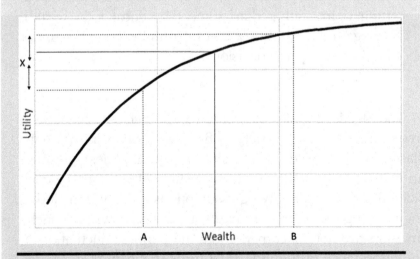

Figure 1.1   A utility curve

associated utility. The loss of utility from potential wealth downside (A) exceeds the gain in utility from an equal potential wealth upside (B), so uncertainty leads to an expected utility (X) less than the utility of the certain outcome. Thus, Utility Theory predicts that individuals are risk averse, that is, a certain outcome is always preferred to an uncertain outcome with the same expected value.

Utility Theory is mathematically elegant, and it is easy to calibrate a utility curve for an individual. From there it is simple to calculate the increase in expected outcome that is required to compensate for any particular level of uncertainty in outcomes. However, whilst Utility Theory is useful to illustrate the concept of risk aversion, it is of little practical use. It is a theory of individual preferences and there is no straightforward way of applying it to a diverse group of stakeholders. Moreover, the focus on total wealth doesn't appear to reflect how people actually approach decisions in real life. Prospect Theory (Kahneman and Tversky (1979)) provides a much better representation of how real people make decisions, based on gains and losses from a concrete starting point, rather than some theoretical total wealth. Once again though, it is a theory of individual choice, not of how groups make decisions.

The idealised notion of well-diversified shareholders, who invest in a very wide variety of firms (and other investment classes such as government debt and commodities), presents an important special case of ownership, which must be considered. If some simplifying assumptions are made (including ignoring the effects of taxes!), it can be shown that such investors are not concerned about the periodic fluctuations in performance of the individual firms in which they invest. Well-diversified shareholders are protected from these routine ups and downs simply by virtue of being so well diversified. Following our earlier discussion, there is *uncertainty* in the performance of individual firms but, in aggregate, there are no consequences for this sort of investor; so, they perceive no *risk*. These idealised owners are therefore concerned only with "systemic risk", that is the extent to which fluctuations in the firms in which they invest co-vary with fluctuations in the market as a whole, known as "beta", as this cannot be mitigated by diversification. Beta is largely determined by the industry sector(s) in which the firm operates, and other strategic choices, so it is not generally relevant to a discussion of risk management such as this one.

Sadly, most of us do have to pay taxes and, in most jurisdictions, taxes can be minimised over the long-term by maintaining profits at a steady level. Exceptional profits in one year may attract higher marginal rates of tax, whilst losses can only generally be carried forward for a few years; so, variability in performance does indeed cost shareholders. Thus, in a world with taxes, variability in performance does present a risk, even to the most well-diversified investors. There are actually a number of other important reasons to minimise variation, including avoiding the "adjustment costs" of continually increasing and reducing capacity, and ensuring that internal funds are always available to respond to opportunities/demands effectively as and when they arise. Critically, the last two arguments apply equally to public sector and not-for-profit organisations.

It is also worth noting that the effect of variations in firm performance is not symmetrical in real life. Large negative swings can result in bankruptcy (and other forms of financial distress), which impose significant costs, both in terms of the loss of business in the run-up to the collapse of a firm and the discounting of the firm's assets (equipment, stocks of goods and raw materials, intangible assets) if they have to be disposed of in a hurry. Large negative variations in performance therefore present a quite separate risk to owners/shareholders, distinct from more modest ups and downs. Once again, even in environments where there are no owners, there are real costs to financial distress.

Finally, many owners do not fit this idealised picture of well-diversified shareholders. Individuals often hold large stakes in particular companies, which represent a significant proportion of their total wealth. In the most extreme cases, entrepreneurs may have all their wealth tied up in a start-up firm, but un-diversified shareholders are present much more widely, even in very large corporations. The uncertainty in the performance of firms does therefore present a real risk to these shareholders.

It should be clear by now that attitudes towards fluctuations in performance are very dependent on the nature of ownership of the organisation. This is a theme that I will return to repeatedly in subsequent chapters.

Senior Management

Senior managers, whatever sector they are operating in, will principally be concerned with avoiding negative outcomes such as loss of employment and/or reputation, typically arising from a failure to meet specific performance targets. These targets have traditionally been linked to accounting measures of performance, but increasingly, at least in the private sector, they may be based on market measures (e.g. share price). As mentioned above, encountering financial distress is an extreme example of a negative outcome that senior managers will be particularly concerned to avoid. Again, from their work talking to practising managers, March and Shapira (1987, p.1407) found that "most managers do not treat uncertainty about positive outcomes as an important aspect of risk". However, in the private sector, this attitude may have changed in recent years as managerial compensation has increasingly included grants of shares and share options, making many senior managers (un-diversified) shareholders in the companies for which they work. There is now an extensive literature about how executive compensation packages, and other factors, drive risk-taking behaviour (see sidebar).

RISK-TAKING SIDEBAR

Whilst it has evolved as a separate strand in the academic literature, the study of risk-taking by executives is, quite clearly, relevant to any discussion of risk management. Much of the literature concerns the effect of executive compensation packages in the private sector on behaviour and, in particular, the use of stock options. A number of studies have found an association between the increasing use of stock options and:

■ High levels of investment in risky activities such as explorative research and development projects, capital expenditure and acquisitions;
■ More extreme performance; and
■ More big losses than big gains.

Other studies have identified additional factors, applicable outside the private sector, that increase executive propensity for risk-taking; these include:

■ Recent good performance (and positive media coverage thereof);
■ More generous CEO severance pay;
■ CEOs who have a private pilot's licence (presented as a proxy for personal propensity for risk-taking); and
■ CEOs from "upper class" backgrounds!

Whilst academic studies have focused on corporations, risk-taking is categorically not confined to the private sector, or to purely financial considerations. Some real examples that I have encountered in the not-for-profit sector include:

■ What likelihood of financial distress for a national governing body of a sport is tolerable in order to enable athletes to qualify for the Olympic Games?
■ What likelihood of death or serious injury to researchers in a university is tolerable to produce a world-class academic journal article?

There are also arguments suggesting that senior managers may experience a negative impact from variability in the performance of their organisation. The simplest argument is that consistent performance is seen as evidence of good management so that managers' reputations will be adversely affected if the organisation's performance is seen to vary more than its peer group. A more subtle line of argument concerns the difficulty of management demonstrating (to investors or other stakeholders) that performance is improving if a general upward trend is overlaid with a lot of "noise".[*]

Lenders, Staff and Other Stakeholders

The risk perspective of lenders is probably the most straightforward of all stakeholder groups: they are only really concerned with the probability of default and their likely losses

---

[*] Of course, the same logic implies that noise could be used to try to obscure a downward trend in performance. Frequent changes of accounting year ends are a classic indicator of attempts to hide underlying problems.

in the event of a default. They do not share in any positive outcomes so these are of no interest to them.

As with senior managers, more junior staff will principally be concerned with negative outcomes such as loss of employment. However, this is more likely to come about through poor performance of the organisation overall, culminating potentially in financial distress, rather than their individual failure to meet targets. Many other stakeholder groups, such as customers and suppliers, will also be concerned with the long-term viability of the organisations with which they interact; thus, their risk perspective will also focus on the likelihood of financial distress.

Other important stakeholder groups, such as regulators and central/local government agencies, may have very specific risk perspectives concerning the organisation's impact on others. Examples could include the risk of not being able to carry out activities deemed essential to critical national infrastructure or the risk of polluting the environment.

Reconciling Conflicting Interests

The risk perspectives of different stakeholder groups will not always be aligned. This was starkly illustrated recently during the Covid-19 pandemic, where many organisations had to balance the impacts on owners, customers and suppliers of suspending operations, with the concerns of staff about their own safety in attending work. When different risk perspectives give rise to conflicting views, how should these be resolved? The classical economic argument is that the conflict should be resolved by financially compensating specific stakeholder groups, and there is some empirical evidence that, for example:

■ People do require higher pay to work in physically dangerous environments; and

■ Senior managers require more generous compensation to take executive roles in organisations where job security is perceived to be poor.

Much of the historical debate on conflicts of interest has focused specifically on the "agency costs", which arise when the interests of owners and managers diverge. This has generally been addressed through a combination of managerial compensation that aligns their interests with the interests of owners, and improved monitoring of managerial actions through enhanced corporate governance and internal control arrangements.

Nevertheless, tensions between different stakeholder groups arising from different risk perspectives will probably persist, but these are no different to the many other tensions that arise in any organisation. Cyert and March (1992, p.164) observed that, in reality, these tensions are generally not resolved through different stakeholder groups compensating each other; indeed, most are not really resolved at all. Coining the phrase "quasi-resolution of conflict", they argue that conflicts are managed through two main mechanisms:

■ "Local rationality"; and
■ "Sequential attention to goals".

Local rationality refers to the practice of delegating goals and decisions to various levels within the organisation. This has the effect of breaking down a complex problem into a number of simpler problems that can be solved at a local level. Local rationality is generally achieved through establishing "acceptable-level decision rules". Once these rules are established, different parts of the organisation can then work independently, knowing that any course of action that complies with these rules is considered to be *satisfactory* to the organisation as a whole. This process of finding acceptable solutions, rather than trying to optimise, is known as *satisficing*. This overall approach is typical of risk management systems, where managers have a degree of delegated responsibility to manage risks within their own area of responsibility, subject to satisfying certain criteria: I will return to this point when looking at risk management systems in detail in Chapter 3. The concept of satisficing will also be central to the practical implementation of a quantitative approach to risk management, which is discussed in Chapters 4, 5 and 6.

The other way in which organisations try to manage conflict is by attending to different goals sequentially. A very obvious example of this is the way in which start-up companies focus on building revenue at first, typically with no attention to profitability, and then, once revenues are deemed sufficient, they try to refocus on generating a profit. In the context of risk management, the attending to different goals may well be a cyclical process. For example, an initial focus on managing risk from the perspective of owners may give way to a focus on managing risk from the customers' perspective (perhaps in response to a quality or reliability issue), which in turn gives way to a focus on managing risk from the perspective of staff members (perhaps in response to a specific safety issue), before returning to a renewed focus on the owners' perspective.

Risk Measures

Given the preceding discussion about the very different stakeholder concepts of risk, it is unsurprising that this has resulted in the use of a wide variety of risk measures in the academic and practitioner literatures. Four of the most important types of risk measures are discussed briefly below: the first two measures are very much focused on quantifying risk at the highest levels within an organisation, whilst the third measure is applied at a local level. I conclude by looking at a risk measure which can be applied at various different levels within an organisation.

Likelihood of Financial Distress

As discussed above, the likelihood of an organisation experiencing financial distress is a key concern to a wide array of stakeholders, including owners/shareholders, senior managers, other staff, lenders, suppliers and customers. Unsurprisingly then, many techniques for modelling the likelihood of financial distress have been developed. Early models were based on accounting measures, typically a combination of measures of profitability, financial leverage and liquidity. More recent models, utilising "Options Theory", are based on market data. There is a fairly straightforward practical trade-off here: measures based on accounting data can be applied to a wide range of organisations (or parts of organisations) but are inherently backward-looking and can only be updated as frequently as accounting data are published, whereas models based on market data can only be applied to quoted companies, but can be updated as frequently as one wishes.

Variability in Outcomes

As discussed above, owners (and potentially senior managers too) may perceive a risk from routine variations in performance, so variance may be one of a number of useful measures of risk in many situations. Measures of variability in performance at the corporate level have been constructed in many different ways, based on both market measures (for publicly listed companies) and, more broadly, accounting measures such as return on assets or return on equity. As well as calculating the variance of the metric of interest, standard deviation* has been widely used too. With some thought, measures of variation (e.g. variability in income or cashflow) can also be applied to individual business units within a larger firm, or to not-for-profit and public sector organisations. As with measures of financial distress though, dependence on accounting data comes at the cost of only being able to update the risk measures relatively infrequently.

Counting Events

The risk measures described above may all seem very remote from the practical aspects of managing risk operationally. At a local level, risks are more often measured in terms of the frequency of occurrence (and, ideally, impact) of particular events, such as IT outages or workplace injuries. As will be explained in Chapter 5, this bottom-up approach is actually the basis of the risk management approach that I advocate, and from which any required measures of risk at the corporate level can be constructed.

Value at Risk

Value at Risk (VaR) came to great prominence as a risk measure in the financial services sector in the 1990s, as an ambitious attempt to express risk in a single number, and has been applied very widely since. The appeal of VaR lies in the simplicity of a single number and in the fact that it can be applied equally to a single investment, a portfolio of investments or an entire organisation. Whilst this terminology harks back to its origins in financial services, "investment" can be interpreted as

---

* Mathematically, the standard deviation is simply the square root of the variance.

any decision to commit resources such as improving IT capabilities, launching an advertising campaign or conducting an R&D project.

VaR is simply a defined percentile of a distribution of outcomes over a given time period; for example, a "1-day 95% VaR" or a "3-month 99% VaR". This is illustrated below with an example of a profit and loss distribution, but the basic principle could be applied to any distribution of outcomes (e.g. the operating surplus of a charity). The values at risk at the 95% and 99% levels are shown in Figure 1.2 (the precise values are $VaR_{95} = £627,000$ and $VaR_{99} = £916,000$).

The discussion thus far has already highlighted the futility of trying to capture risk in a single number: at best VaR may capture risk from the perspective of one or more stakeholder groups in any given situation. That argument applies equally to any individual risk measure, but VaR suffers from a more fundamental limitation in that it completely ignores the shape of the loss distribution above the chosen percentile: it does not differentiate between different "tail distributions" of extremely high losses. Concerns have also been raised about

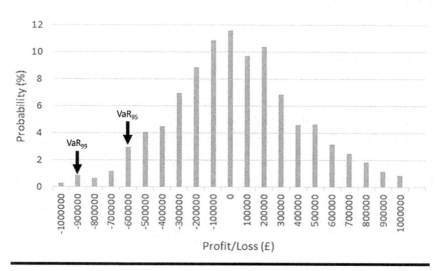

Figure 1.2   An Example of Value at Risk

the potential that the VaR figure becomes confused in people's minds with a maximum possible loss. Many commentators have cited these two issues, both individually and in combination with each other, as contributory factors in the credit crunch of 2007-2008, and the proponents of VaR are now somewhat less ambitious in their claims.

Notwithstanding these criticisms of VaR itself, I will return to look in detail at many such distributions of outcomes in subsequent chapters.

Categorisation of Risks

In concluding this discussion of risk, it is worth looking briefly at the categorisation of risk. Such categorisations are of particular utility in the process of identifying risks (this will be discussed in more detail in Chapter 5). Many categorisations or typologies have been proposed over recent years; most of these are based on the perceived source of the risk as in the "PESTEL"/"7 S's" categorisation of external and internal risks shown in Table 1.1.

Table 1.1   "PESTEL" and "7 S's" Risk Categorisations

External Sources of Risk – "PESTEL"	Internal Sources of Risk – "7 S's"
Political	Systems
Economic/Markets	Structure
Social	Strategy
Technological	Skills
Environmental / Ethical	Staff
Legal	Style
	Shared Culture

However, the most important distinction in terms of managing risk is the division between those risks which the organisation believes it has a competitive advantage in bearing and are taken voluntarily in the pursuit of higher returns and those risks where there is no perceived competitive advantage but are accepted as part of doing business. Merton (2005) calls these "value-adding" and "passive" risks, respectively. Fundamentally, this book is concerned with the management of passive risks. However, in an ideal world, decisions to accept value-adding risks would be taken on exactly the same basis as decisions to manage passive risks.

Summary

I proposed that risk exists where uncertainty about the future has consequences for an individual or group, whether or not that uncertainty is quantifiable. Risk is usually characterised as a combination of the likelihood of an uncertain event taking place and the impact (on relevant stakeholder groups) if it does.

Risk is not a one-dimensional construct. In most situations different stakeholder groups will perceive risk differently: managing risk may require difficult trade-offs between the interests of different stakeholder groups. In common with other organisational tensions, potential conflict may be managed through a combination of local rationality and sequential attention to goals.

Many different risk measures have been used to capture these different risk perspectives: in many situations, multiple risk measures will be required. Risk measures constructed from market data have the advantage of being forward-looking and being able to be updated frequently, but can only be applied to publicly listed companies.

In determining how to manage risks it is important to distinguish between value-adding risks taken voluntarily in the pursuit of achieving higher returns and passive risks that are merely accepted as a cost of doing business.

References

Bernstein P, 1996, *Against the Gods: The Remarkable Story of Risk*, New York, NY: John Wiley & Sons.

Chittenden J, 2006, *Risk Management Based on M_O_R: A Management Guide*, Zaltbommel: Van Haren.

Cyert and March, 1992, *A Behavioral Theory of the Firm*, 2nd Edition, Malden, MA: Blackwell.

ISO, 2002, *ISO/IEC Guide 73 – Risk Management Vocabulary*, Geneva: International Organization for Standardization.

Kahneman D and Tversky A, 1979, Prospect Theory: An Analysis of Decision Under Risk, *Econometrica*, 47: 263–291.

Knight F, 1964, *Risk, Uncertainty and Profit*, New York: Century Press. (Originally published 1921).

March J and Shapira Z, 1987, Managerial Perspectives on Risk and Risk Taking, *Management Science*, 33(11): 1404–1418.

Markowitz H, 1952, Portfolio Selection, *Journal of Finance*, 7: 77–91.

Merton R, 2005, You Have More Capital Than You Think, *Harvard Business Review*, 83(11): 84–94.

Chapter 2

Why Do We Try to Manage Risk?

Some readers might view this question as being trivial or even meaningless. On the one hand, in disciplines such as health and safety, risk reduction is seen as an end in itself in the pursuit of "zero accidents". At the other extreme, the argument that idealised well-diversified shareholders can insulate themselves from any company-specific risks simply by diversifying their portfolio was discussed in Chapter 1. In these idealised circumstances, any attempts to manage firm-specific risks are a waste of resources and should be rejected. Most of us probably take a pragmatic position somewhere in between these two extremes: some amount of risk management is a good thing, but it can go too far.

In the following sections I look at some of the reasons that one might wish to (try to) manage risk, namely:

- Improving expected outcomes;
- Reducing the likelihood of extreme events;
- Reducing variability in outcomes;
- Demonstrating good corporate governance; and
- Compulsion.

DOI: 10.4324/9781003225157-2

I also look briefly at why, despite all of these arguments in favour of risk management, so many organisations still do little or nothing. The chapter finishes by summarising a significant body of empirical research into why organisations manage risk and which types of organisations manage risk, and by reviewing to what extent the empirical evidence supports theory.

Improving Expected Outcomes

As I have stated before, decisions about risk management should be taken on the same basis, return on investment, as any other business decisions. The most obvious justification for managing a risk, or portfolio of risks, is that the proposed actions will simply improve the expected outcomes for the organisation. This argument is completely neglected in many standard texts on risk management, where the focus is on financial risks with an essentially symmetrical distribution of positive and negative outcomes. But it is an important motivation in the management of operational risks, where one is generally concerned only with potential losses.

For example, loss of productivity through staff absence due to illness is a risk to organisations in all sectors. If:

- An organisation with 100 staff members is experiencing an average of seven days of staff absence per year through influenza, at an estimated total cost of £2000; and
- The cost of offering flu vaccination to all 100 staff members is only £1000;

then a vaccination programme is clearly justified on the basis of a very straightforward return on investment. In general, such an improvement in expected outcomes will benefit all stakeholder groups; however, the financial savings are ultimately distributed. In this particular example, everybody's interests are also aligned as staff have the opportunity* to receive a vaccination for free (which they might otherwise have to pay for), and customers benefit from reduced disruption to operations from staff absence.

This example is so obvious that it may appear trivial, but it highlights a critical point: it is only possible to calculate the return on investment because suitable data (on staff absence due to flu and the cost to the organisation of this) are available. As I have already mentioned, and will reiterate many times again throughout the book, effective risk management is all about gathering and analysing the right data. Generally, the arguments for risk management will not be quite so clear-cut. Often investment will be required upfront (e.g. investing in improved IT infrastructure) in order to deliver uncertain savings over a period of years; but this is fundamentally no different to making decisions about marketing campaigns, R&D initiatives or any other long-term investment with uncertain returns.

Reducing the Likelihood of Extreme Events

Another powerful argument for managing risk, which also applies across all sectors, is to reduce the risk of a very large loss, particularly one that could result in financial distress for the organisation, or which could prevent it from carrying on business as usual. Indeed, Cyert and March (1992, p.9) propose maximising the long-term probability of survival of the organisation as an explicit goal of entrepreneurial owners. The likelihood of financial distress is also the key concern of

---

* This is obviously different to a situation where staff members are compelled to receive the vaccination.

lenders and will impact very directly on the availability and cost of debt finance. It is embedded in credit ratings and credit scoring models, so it is relatively straightforward to calculate a direct benefit (to any organisation which relies on debt funding) from reducing the likelihood of financial distress. For some organisations the retention of a particular credit rating is also very important for reputational reasons.* The potential for extreme losses to lead to reductions in the workforce is a significant concern for staff, which may impose costs indirectly by affecting how easy it is to recruit people and the wages that they demand. Any concerns about the long-term viability of the organisation will also affect relationships with customers and suppliers, and may impact on both their willingness to do business and the prices that they are willing to pay/charge. Clearly though, these indirect costs are more difficult to quantify, and more open to challenge.

Ultimately, if losses result in bankruptcy, there will be considerable destruction of value as raw materials, finished goods and plant and equipment are all sold off at discounted rates. Intangible assets, such as brand, may also be impaired. Critically, staff will lose their jobs, potentially without any compensation, and may suffer months of financial hardship as they seek new employment. Customers may also be seriously impacted if they are heavily reliant on the organisation for a particular product or service, and suppliers suddenly have to find new buyers for their products and services. If arguments based on improving expected outcomes are not sufficient to demonstrate a business case for a risk management intervention, then reducing the likelihood of extreme losses, and particularly the likelihood of bankruptcy, is typically the next most compelling argument.

---

* In regulated industries such as banking and insurance, being able to demonstrate a reduced likelihood of extreme losses will also reduce the amount of regulatory capital required to support a given volume of business.

Within the public and not-for-profit sectors, there may also be an imperative to reduce the likelihood of non-financial extreme events. Any failure to deliver services that breaches the organisation's statutory obligations could have very significant financial impacts, and even just failing to meet the expectations of politicians or the public can result in significant reputational damage.

Crises and "Black-Swans"

Within a general discussion of extreme outcomes, it is important to specifically address the subject of catastrophic events or "crises", including completely unpredictable "black-swan" (Taleb 2007) events. The black-swan terminology has been applied very commonly in the field of operational risks, the Eyjafjallajökull volcanic eruption in 2010 being a prime example. But the term has also been applied to financial events such as "Black Monday" in 1987, when US markets fell by over 20% in a day, and the "Credit Crunch" of 2007-2008. Much application of the black-swan label is completely inappropriate, confusing an individual's (or a number of individuals') failure to predict an event with a fundamental impossibility to predict the event. For instance, whilst the specific mode of attack on 9/11 was very unusual, it is completely incorrect to say that a terrorist attack on the Twin Towers was a black-swan, as a vehicle bomb under the North Tower killed six people (and injured over 1,000) in 1993. Some commentators even applied the term black-swan to the Covid-19 pandemic, even though many worse pandemics have occurred historically (and, sadly, may continue to do so).

Such low-probability/high-impact events pose a number of significant challenges for risk management, which will be discussed at various points throughout the book; and I will return specifically to the issue of crises in Chapter 8. For now,

I just present a brief summary of the challenges. The first problem arises in identifying these highly unlikely events in the first place. Having identified them, there is then a further significant challenge in gathering data on what are, by definition, very unusual events, and, following the quantitative approach advocated in this book, modelling the impact of them with very limited data. Finally, in the context of this chapter, one is primarily interested in the effect of such events (or the fear of such events) on risk management behaviour. In the realm of very low-probability hazards, people tend to react by either being overly cautious or extremely risk-seeking. This dichotomy of responses when dealing with very low probabilities was elegantly illustrated by an experiment on insurance-buying (see sidebar). I will look at some specific data on the incidence of "crises" and the effect on managers' behaviours towards the end of this chapter.

INSURANCE BUYING SIDEBAR

McClelland et al. (1993) conducted a series of experiments based on purchasing insurance to investigate people's perceptions of risk. As with much research, there is the important caveat that the experimental subjects were undergraduate students in the United States; but they were financially incentivised to carefully consider their responses.

The experiment was conducted in multiple rounds, with probabilities of the risk event ranging from 0.01 to 0.9 (ten rounds were conducted at each probability); in each case, the subject stood to lose $4 if the event occurred. In each round, an auction was held to establish how much each subject would be willing to pay to insure against this event. At high probabilities (greater than 0.5), bids are tightly clustered around the expected value of the loss (e.g. $2.40 for a 0.6 probability of a $4 loss). As the probability decreases towards 0.1, the spread of bids increases; but there is still a pronounced peak around the expected value. Finally, at a probability of 0.01, bids are widely spread with two peaks in the distribution: one at twice the expected value and one at zero. As can be seen in Figure 2.1, 45% of respondents were willing to pay significantly more than the insurance was worth (whilst 26% were not prepared to pay anything at all)

Interestingly, whilst many experimental subjects consistently bid above or below the expected value throughout all ten rounds at a probability of 0.01, some people varied between high and low bids over the course of the experiment. A series of further rounds with an event probability of 0.01 were conducted with different subjects, but the loss for each event was increased to $40: once again there were distinct peaks at twice the expected value and zero. The results of these experiments suggest that, when faced with low-probability hazards, people react in one of two ways:

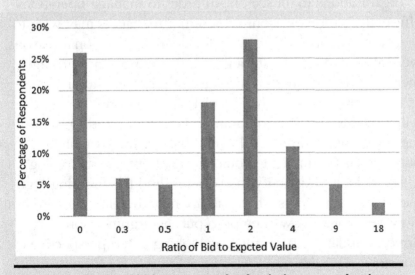

Figure 2.1   Ratio of bid to expected value in insurance-buying experiment (probability of loss = 0.01).

they either completely dismiss them or worry too much about them. If this is the case in an experimental setting where probabilities are precisely known, one would expect even greater divergence in willingness to pay in a real-life situation where probabilities can only be very roughly estimated.

Reducing Variability in Outcomes

A number of reasons why variability in outcomes is undesirable were discussed in Chapter 1. Within the private sector, variability imposes some costs (e.g. increased taxes) for even the most well-diversified shareholders; in addition, less well-diversified investors (e.g. entrepreneurial owners) will experience a loss in their personal utility from any variability. More broadly, maintaining a degree of stability is important to organisations in all sectors, in order to manage operations efficiently. Various reasons why senior managers may wish to reduce variability in outcomes, for their own personal reasons, were also mentioned, although, ideally, governance arrangements should ensure that managers are not able to engage in risk management activities solely for their own benefit (I will return to this specific point in Chapters 3 and 4). Whilst these various arguments all agree that reducing variability in outcomes is desirable, it should be apparent that it is going to be difficult to quantify the benefits, and the resulting arguments for managing such variability may therefore lack impact. However, I shall now attempt to put the argument on a firmer foundation, beginning by looking at the perspective of investors.

Historically, stock market investments have out-performed government bonds over the long term; so, presumably, if variability of outcomes was not a problem everybody would invest their money in the stock market. Continuing this line of argument, one can try to quantify how much people (on average) require to compensate them for the variability in stock market returns. Data from the US stock market over the period 1939-1990 show that somebody who invested in a portfolio mimicking the market as a whole (something tracking the S&P 500 would be a reasonable approximation to this) would have experienced a standard deviation of 21.6% in annual returns to their portfolio, in return for which they would have received an excess return (over returns from a risk-free investment, such as government bonds) of 11.5%/year. This would suggest that investors, in aggregate, require an additional 1% in expected returns for each additional 2% of standard deviation in returns from an investment. Looking at this another way, investors are willing to accept roughly a 30% chance annually that their portfolio will underperform a risk-free investment, falling to less than a 10% chance over a five-year period and less than 1% over a ten-year period. Clearly, the time horizons of investors are critical in any consideration of their risk perspective.

Figures from the UK stock market for the period 1983-1987 (see Table 2.1) show a broadly similar ratio between standard deviation and excess return, but the relationship completely breaks down in subsequent five-year periods.

Table 2.1   Analysis of FTSE All Share Returns 1983-2012

	Standard Deviation (%)	*Excess Return (%)*
1983-1987	20.4	8.9
1988-1992	17.0	-3.5
1993-1997	11.4	7.1
1997-2002	16.3	-13.0
2003-2007	9.7	7.1
2008-2012	17.0	-0.1

So, it would appear that investors' risk perspectives are actually very dependent on the prevailing economic conditions: in a downturn with few profitable investment opportunities, they may be prepared to tolerate much greater risks for very limited returns. But at least the analysis above gives an order of magnitude: it appears that investors are not going to demand any more than 1% additional return for each 1% of standard deviation. Putting that in a risk management framing, one can conclude that investors will be willing to sacrifice no more than 1% of expected return to reduce standard deviation of returns by 1%. It is important to bear in mind also the point made in Chapter 1 that apart from entrepreneurial owners, most investors will be able to reduce much of this variation simply by diversifying their portfolio; so, they will be prepared to pay significantly less to reduce variability in returns for a single firm.

In principle, one can explore the risk perspective of managers empirically in a similar fashion, from firm-level studies based on accounting returns. However, these firm-level studies are relatively rare and there are a number of important considerations in the design of these studies, such as what risk measure(s) to include, how long a period to calculate these risk measures over, and what time gap to allow between the measurement of risk and the measurement of returns. Different studies have therefore found quite a range of results. My own research in this area on firms in the UK FTSE 350 (see Annex A for a more detailed discussion) looked at the relationship between a wide range of risk measures calculated over a five-year period and the return on equity in the year following that five-year period. It is important to note that the study time frame included the credit crunch of 2007-2008. In the comparatively benign environment that prevailed pre-2007, it was found that a 1% increase in the standard deviation of return on assets was associated with a subsequent 3-5% increase in return on equity. However, as the global economy

crashed, this risk premium largely disappeared. As with investors, it appears that the risk perspective of managers is very
dependent on prevailing conditions.

Demonstrating Good Corporate Governance

As discussed above, managing the likelihood of extreme
events is critical in securing and maintaining the confidence of
external stakeholders and maintaining an organisation's reputation. However, there is also now a broader argument that
following generally agreed good practice for risk management
(see Chapter 3) is seen as evidence of good corporate governance, and therefore enhances an organisation's reputation.
Thus, being able to demonstrate adherence to good practice,
e.g. by certifying to a relevant ISO standard, may provide
reputational benefits over and above the direct costs of mitigating any specific risks. These benefits could include the
ability to win new business, improved relationships with customers and suppliers, the ability to recruit and retain the best
people and the ability to attract grants or institutional investors. Again, many of these benefits may be very difficult to
quantify and it will be hard to construct a compelling business
case. However, in certain circumstances, the ability to win
grants or contracts alone may provide a very straightforward
cost-benefit argument. For example, there has been a trend
in the United Kingdom over recent years towards making the
ability to demonstrate a formalised approach to specific risk
management activities, such as business continuity management and/or information security management, a prerequisite
for bidding for many contracts, particularly in the public sector. Even if risk management is not an explicit requirement to
bid, it may be an important part of the technical evaluation
of bids. If an organisation operates in such an environment,
then it should be relatively easy to calculate a direct benefit of

implementation in terms of an increased likelihood of winning tenders and/or being able to charge more for contracts.

Compulsion

It is also important to mention that some organisations are compelled to engage in certain risk management activities for legal or regulatory reasons in many jurisdictions. For example, within the United Kingdom:

- A basic level of risk reporting is required under the *Companies Act 2006 (Strategic Report and Directors' Report) Regulations 2013* for all publicly listed companies; and
- The emergency services and various other government agencies (known as "Tier-1 Responders") are required to undertake planning for emergencies under the *Civil Contingencies Act 2004.*

Specific risk management requirements also apply to certain industry sectors; for instance, large banks and insurance companies across the world are required to comply with Basel III and Solvency II, respectively. However, even when organisations are compelled to undertake risk management, there are still important decisions to make about how to manage risk and which specific risk management actions to take, which will be informed by the arguments above about why one might seek to manage risk.

Why Do We Not Manage Risk?

Despite the many and varied arguments for investing in risk management outlined above, it would appear that very many people* still choose to do little or nothing (I look at some figures on uptake of risk management in the next section). It is therefore worth considering briefly some of the reasons why risk management may be neglected.

Once again, Cyert and March (1992, p.169) provide some useful insights in this regard. One of the authors' key concepts is the idea of "problemistic search", that is to say that organisational changes are usually made in direct response to a failure to meet a specific goal (e.g. an annual revenue or profit target), rather than as the result of some idealised process of continuous improvement. It is difficult to envisage how something as abstract as a lack of risk management would be seen as an obvious solution to the failure to achieve a specific goal. This problem is compounded by the authors' observation that, having identified a problem, people generally engage in "simplistic search" for solutions, rather than a thorough root-cause analysis. Thus, people tend to identify solutions which are:

- "In the neighbourhood of the problem symptom"; and
- "In the neighbourhood of the current alternative".

So, for example, if members of IT staff become aware of a problem with the downtime of systems, their search for solutions will most likely focus on technical fixes, which are both close to the symptom and similar to existing solutions that they have in place. It seems highly unlikely that a simplistic search in response to an IT issue would conclude that the organisation needs to have a (better) risk management system, which will ultimately provide high-level visibility of the impacts of outages and thus generate senior management

---

* I say "people" quite deliberately: organisations do not make decisions. I have seen dramatic changes in approach to risk management in organisations as a direct result of a new CEO or other executive.

commitment to providing the resources to address the root causes of the problem.

Finally, and crucially, the authors highlight that, when budgets are tight, activities with weak linkage to concrete organisational outcomes (principally revenue and profit) are the most vulnerable to being cut. They cite the specific example of R&D spending, but the argument is equally applicable to risk management. One of the attractions of the approach to risk management outlined in this book is that risk management decisions are presented in the same way (return on investment) as any other business decision, rather than as some discrete class of decisions that are not directly linked to the outcomes for the organisation as a whole.

The literature on the diffusion of innovations also sheds light on the problem of underinvestment in risk management. "Preventive Innovations" are defined as a new idea that an individual adopts now in order to lower the probability of some unwanted future event: common examples include the purchase of insurance and following public health advice. Preventive innovations are different to the more usual "Incremental Innovations" (such as investing in new technology or new ways of doing business to improve productivity) in two, very important ways:

■ The desired consequence is distant in time; and
■ The unwanted event is difficult to perceive, so the associated benefit is less salient.

As a result of these factors, the diffusion of preventive innovations is observed to be particularly slow. This argument could be applied both to the overall decision to implement risk management across an organisation and to individual risk management decisions at lower levels within the organisation.

I have already highlighted the potential problem that senior managers could invest in risk management to benefit themselves (e.g. to reduce the likelihood of missing targets), even if these interventions were not in the interests of other stakeholder groups (e.g. owners). In the context of the current discussion, one must also recognise the possibility that senior managers may not invest enough (from the perspective of other stakeholder groups) in risk management because it does not benefit them personally. Put very crudely if, for instance, a CEO is intending to be in post only for three to five years, and believes that the likelihood of a major data breach is less than 10% annually, how motivated are they going to be to reduce day-to-day profits (on which they are measured and rewarded) in order to invest in information security, when they believe there is at least a 50% chance that they will never have to deal with the consequences. Indeed, traditionally, one of the arguments for purchasing insurance was that the directors of the company expected that the insurance company would perform an oversight function in ensuring that senior managers manage risks appropriately, in the best interests of the owners.

It would appear then that, in many ways, the odds are stacked against investment in risk management! This observation emphasises once again the importance of re-casting risk management decisions as normal business decisions, rather than a completely separate category of decisions which can apparently be neglected at will.

Empirical Evidence

I now turn to look at whether there is any empirical evidence to support the theoretical arguments for managing risk discussed in the preceding sections. Obviously, all organisations manage risk: in addition to whatever informal risk management that we carry out as individuals, most jurisdictions require the purchase of certain lines of insurance (such as public liability) and compliance with legislation around, for instance, health and safety and environmental protection. In researching risk management, one is therefore really concerned with the steps that organisations take, in some sort of formalised way, over and above what is legally required.

Different studies have used many different proxies for the adoption of risk management, including the (voluntary) purchase of insurance, the use of options to mitigate specific risks, the establishment of a Chief Risk Officer role (or equivalent), public statements about risk management, the employment of risk management professionals, and certification to ISO standards. I first look at some data on the overall adoption of risk management, before looking at which sorts of organisations are more inclined to manage risk. I conclude this section by looking at empirical data on the incidence of crises and whether this has any effect on attitudes to risk management.

How Many Organisations Manage Risk?

The answer to this question depends entirely on where one sets the bar. At the very highest level, very few organisations go as far as certifying to any of the relevant ISO standards. For example, as of the end of 2020, there were only 2,205 "valid certifications" globally to *ISO 22301: Security and Resilience – Business Continuity Management Systems – Requirements*, and only 44,486 "valid certifications" to *ISO 27001: Information Technology – Security Techniques – Information Security Management Systems – Requirements** (ISO, 2021). At the next level down, looking at the employment of risk management professionals, as of 2011, 15% of FTSE 350 companies employed a member of the *Business Continuity Institute*, whilst 13% employed a member of the *Institute of Risk*

---

* ISO 31000: Risk Management – Guidance and Best Practice is guidance rather than a standard against which an organisation can be certified.

Management.[*] Turning to analyses of what organisations say
and do publicly about risk management, Bertinetti et al. (2013)
concluded that by 2011, 61% of a sample of 300 European
firms had "adopted" Enterprise Risk Management (ERM).[†]
Similarly, Sprcic et al. (2016) judged that by 2012, 68% of a
sample of US firms had "adopted" ERM.

Which Organisations Manage Risk?

There is reasonable consensus from most studies, including
those looking at the purchase of insurance, the use of options
and the appointment of a Chief Risk Officer, that organisations with a higher probability of financial distress are more
likely to engage in risk management. This would support the
argument outlined above - that the risk of financial distress is
a key concern to multiple stakeholder groups (including owners, staff members, lenders and customers). Some studies also
found that the cost of financial distress, which is only really
a risk to owners, was a driver for risk management; but the
evidence here is much less conclusive.

Direct evidence that a desire to reduce volatility is associated with the adoption of risk management is largely derived
from studies looking at managerial incentives. Tufano's (1996,
p.1097) classic study of the North American gold-mining
industry found that "firms whose managers hold more stock
manage more gold price risk". Replicating these findings has
become more complicated as managerial incentive packages
have evolved (see sidebar on risk taking in Chapter 1), but a
more recent study did find clear evidence that the purchase of

---

[*] These percentages are not mutually exclusive – some firms employed members
of both institutions – so the overall proportion of firms employing risk management professionals is less than 28%.

[†] Enterprise Risk Management is discussed in detail in Chapter 3.

property insurance amongst Chinese firms was being driven by managerial self-interest.

It is also worth noting that a small number of studies have found a positive association between the proportion of institutional ownership and risk management. This would tend to support the argument that risk management is, in some cases, being driven by a desire to demonstrate good corporate governance, in order to attract or retain institutional investors.

Thus, theory and observation appear to align pretty well in explaining why organisations seek to manage risk. Aside from improving expected outcomes, the most compelling argument for risk management appears to derive from reducing the likelihood of extreme events. The benefits of reducing variability in outcomes are also real, but very dependent on the nature of ownership, the prevailing economic environment and how managers are incentivised. Finally, the nature of ownership may also indirectly drive interest in risk management as part of a wider corporate governance agenda.

The Incidence of Catastrophic Events and "Crises"

There is a powerful argument that a genuine "crisis" is, by definition, unique; so, in attempting any sort of quantitative study, one is really applying a much looser definition, often based on the level of impact of the event. An example of this is Ernst & Young (2002), which found that 40% of the 1,000 largest firms globally experienced at least one drop in value of greater than 30% in a single month in the preceding five-year period, and 5% of firms experienced a drop of greater than 50%. Coleman (2004, p.4) took a more systematic approach to a study of corporate crises in Australia, defining a crisis as a "single incident or issue which escalates uncontrollably and causes such serious damage to the assets, reputation and performance of an organisation that its viability is threatened". Applying this definition, he found 55 examples of corporate crises reported in the media over a 12-year period from 1990 to 2002, including product recalls, extortion, mass casualty incidents and criminal acts. It is interesting to note that 27% of the firms that experienced crises in this period had disappeared by the time that the article was written in 2004. More recently, PwC (2019) found that 69% of a global sample of 2,000 firms experienced at least one crisis* in the previous five years, with 45% experiencing more than one and 7% experiencing more than five.

There is also some evidence from such studies that the experience of extreme events influences risk management behaviour. Steelhenge (2014, p.5) found that 29% of a sample of 375 firms (primarily UK-based and including a number of SMEs) had developed a "crisis management plan" as a direct result of "A crisis, operational incident or near-miss". Similarly, Sadiq and Graham (2016) found that experience of previous natural disasters was a significant predictor of "Employer-Level Preparedness Activities".†

Summary

There are a number of different ways in which risk management activities may confer a benefit on different stakeholder

---

* For the purposes of the PwC survey, a crisis is defined as a situation that "Is triggered by significant internal and/or external factors or escalation of smaller incident(s); has an enterprise-wide, multi-functional impact; creates disruption in normal business operations; and has the potential for reputational harm/ damage".

† This was a composite measure of emergency preparedness comprising designating a person to be in charge of disaster planning/management, developing an emergency/contingency plan, developing a mutual aid agreement with other organisations, purchasing hazard insurance, updating emergency employee contact lists, obtaining an emergency generator and obtaining a back-up communication system.

groups. A single risk intervention may impact positively in a number of different ways.

The most straightforward way to justify a risk management intervention is usually that it improves expected outcomes. If this argument on its own is not sufficient to justify the investment required, then reducing the likelihood of extreme events is generally the next most straightforward approach.

Reducing variation in outcomes is also of benefit to some stakeholder groups, but the value of this depends both on the nature of ownership and the prevailing economic conditions.

The other potential benefits of risk mitigation will often be very difficult to quantify but, in some environments, the need to demonstrate good practice in risk management in order to win contracts or grants can provide a compelling business case on its own.

Quite separately to all of the above, previous experience of, or fear of, a catastrophic incident or crisis may be an important driver for investment in risk management.

References

Bertinetti G, Cavezzali E and Gardenal G, 2013, The Effect of Enterprise Risk Management Implementation on the Firm Value of European Companies, Universita Ca Foscari Venezia Department of Management Working Paper Series, 10/2013.

Coleman L, 2002, The Frequency and Cost of Corporate Crises, *Journal of Contingencies and Crisis Management*, 12(1): 2–13.

Cyert and March, 1992, *A Behavioral Theory of the Firm*, 2nd Edition, Malden, MA: Blackwell.

Ernst & Young, 2002, *Risks That Matter: Sudden Increases and Decreases in Shareholder Value and the Implications for CEOs*, Ernst & Young/Oxford Metrica. Available at http://www.oxford-metrica.com/public/cms/files/599/02repcomey.pdf (downloaded 21/09/21).

ISO, 2021, *ISO Survey 2020*. Available at https://www.iso.org/the-iso -survey.html (downloaded 22/09/21).

McClelland G, Schulze W and Coursey D, 1993, Insurance for Low-Probability Hazards: A Bimodal Response to Unlikely Events, *Journal of Risk and Uncertainty*, 7: 95–116.

PwC, 2019, *Crisis Preparedness as the next Competitive Advantage: Learning from 4,500 Crises*, PwC. Available at https://www.pwc .com/ee/et/publications/pub/pwc-global-crisis-survey-2019.pdf (downloaded 21/09/21).

Sadiq A-A and Graham J, 2016, Exploring the Predictors of Organizational Preparedness for Natural Disasters, *Risk Analysis*, 36(5): 1040–1053.

Sprcic D, Zagar M, Sevic Z and Marc M, 2016, Does Enterprise Risk Management Influence Market Value - A Long-Term Perspective, *Risk Management: An International Journal*, 18(2–3): 65–88.

Steelhenge, 2014, *Preparing for Crisis: Safeguarding your Future*, Steelhenge. (Following the takeover of Steelhenge by Register Larkin, and subsequent takeover of Register Larkin by Deloitte; this document appears to be no longer available).

Taleb N, 2007, *The Black Swan*, London: Allen Lane.

Tufano P, 1996, Who Manages Risk? An Empirical Examination of Risk Management Practices in the Gold Mining Industry, *Journal of Finance*, 51(4): 1097–1137.

Chapter 3

Risk Management Systems

I have been, and will continue to be, critical of what I have characterised as the compliance approach to risk management, or what Power (2007, p.179) describes as "the administrative positivism of the accountant and auditor". That is not because there is nothing of value in any of the standards and guidance documents to which compliance is sought, rather it is because this compliance approach:

- Has driven the development of risk management as a separate, specialised activity within organisations (often under an overall corporate governance umbrella);
- Has led to the very widespread use of inappropriate, qualitative techniques because they are (perceived to be) easier to formalise, document and audit than quantitative approaches; and
- Results in a focus on the risks themselves, rather than the positive actions that can be undertaken to mitigate them.

DOI: 10.4324/9781003225157-3

This chapter begins by discussing the development of the overall concept of *integrated risk management*, and reviewing some of the empirical evidence on how well these ideas have been implemented in practice. I then look critically at the operationalisation of integrated risk management in one particular form, *ISO 31000: Risk Management - Guidance and Best Practice* (ISO, 2009, 2018). Whilst there is much to agree with in ISO 31000, I will focus on the areas where I strongly believe that different methods are required; this provides the foundations for a detailed description of my proposed approach to risk management in the next three chapters. This chapter concludes with a brief discussion of risk displacement and risk compensation.

Integrated Risk Management

At the core of all modern good practice guidance is a move away from risk management's historical focus on managing specific risks, towards an integrated, enterprise-wide approach to managing risk. This has been variously described as "Integrated Risk Management", "Strategic Risk Management" and, most commonly, as "Enterprise Risk Management" (ERM). To avoid confusion with the specific implementation of ERM laid out in *Enterprise Risk Management* (COSO, 2004), I will refer to the generic concept as integrated risk management throughout.

The Aims of Integrated Risk Management

The core idea of integrated risk management is to manage the risks that an organisation faces coherently as a portfolio, in pursuit of the organisation's overall strategy. Recalling Merton (2005), this includes, at least in the private sector, both "value-adding risks" that are taken voluntarily in the pursuit of higher returns, and "passive risks" where the organisation has no competitive advantage. Integrated risk management therefore involves:

■ Collating and aggregating risk information from across the organisation;
■ Applying a consistent approach to managing passive risks across the organisation as a whole, including embedding risk management processes within normal business planning; and
■ Applying the same risk perspectives to the consideration of value-adding risks as and when opportunities arise.

These overall aims are now very widely accepted, but the ability of specific approaches to integrated risk management, particularly ERM, to achieve them are hotly debated. For example, Power (2007, p.98) argues that "ERM is an illusion of control which may be a necessary illusion because it reconstitutes a possible unity for a fragmented management field". Other writers have specifically criticised ERM as being too internally focused and ignoring the inter-relatedness of modern supply chains. Whether risk management activities actually achieve what they set out to do will be a recurring theme throughout the rest of this book. In the next section I begin this discussion by looking briefly at some empirical evidence on the success of implementation of formal risk management systems.

Implementation of Integrated Risk Management Systems

Empirical studies into the implementation of risk management systems have highlighted significant practical problems in realising a truly integrated, enterprise-wide approach to risk management. Arena et al. (2010) examined the success of implementation by conducting long-term case studies of three Italian companies that claimed to have adopted ERM. They found much confusion amongst the staff members that they spoke to about what ERM actually involved, and found that, in two out of three firms, pre-existing approaches to risk management remained in widespread use and were not in any way linked to the new ERM programme. As one interviewee (p.667) memorably puts it: "We did not need an instrument for evaluating risks; we know perfectly well where our risks lie. They have not changed since I've been here, and all of us know what our risks are and where to find the information to obtain a picture of the future". Supporting the earlier discussion of different stakeholder risk perspectives, the authors suggest that the persistence of these legacy approaches stems primarily from "differing risk rationalities and their potential to challenge the conceptualization of uncertainty" (p. 673). If two out of the three organisations in the study have failed to reconcile these competing risk perspectives amongst different stakeholder groups, it seems highly unlikely that there is any consensus on other aspects of risk management.

Turning to the success of implementing other approaches to risk management, Green (2006) conducted a study into the degree to which business continuity management (BCM) had been implemented in different business units within HBOS, a large UK-based banking group, and found wide and persistent variation. Following the 9/11 attacks, the bank had introduced an annual BCM benchmarking exercise. Each of the bank's 39 business units was asked to self-assess the completeness of their BCM programme along six dimensions.* Each dimension comprised a number of specific questions to be rated

---

* The dimensions were "Risk Analysis", "Business Impact Analysis", "Strategy Definition", "Emergency Response", "Detailed Plan Implementation" and "Testing".

on a four-point scale (0-3). These scores were then weighted (weightings ranged from 1 to 8), summed and converted into a percentage of the maximum possible score, to give an overall measure of the completeness of BCM implementation within that business unit. When the benchmarking exercise was first conducted in 2001, overall scores across the 39 business units ranged from 31% to 91%! By the time of the 2005 benchmarking the average score had improved significantly, the mean had increased from 60% to 85%, but there was still very considerable variation between business units. Whilst the business units scoring worst in 2001 had all improved (the minimum score was now 51%), the inter-quartile range (i.e. the difference between the 25th percentile and the 75th percentile) had actually increased from 41% to 42%. It is also worth noting that five business units actually achieved a lower score in 2005 than they had done in 2001.

Roberts and Stephens (2009) observed a very similar pattern of cross-sectional variation in the maturity of BCM across the Medical Research Council's 26 UK-based units. This strongly suggests that the problem of inconsistency in adoption is not limited to the financial services sector, nor even the private sector in general. The same barriers to implementing risk management at the corporate level, that were discussed in Chapter 2, apply also at each business unit and departmental level. Just because a decision has been made corporately to implement (a particular approach to), risk management does not mean that everybody within the organisation will actively embrace it.

ISO 31000

As an international standard, ISO 31000 has been very influential in risk management practice since publication of the first version in 2009. As with other approaches to integrated risk management, it is not without its critics (see, for example Leitch (2010)), but its widespread use makes it the ideal basis for discussion. In common with most good practice guidance, ISO 31000 comprises two main components: a *risk management framework* and a *risk management process*. These are discussed below.

The Risk Management Framework

ISO 31000 (2018) provides detailed guidance on what is required by way of a risk management framework under the following headings:

- Leadership and commitment;
- Integration;
- Design;
- Implementation;
- Evaluation; and
- Improvement.

Together, these lay the groundwork to allow the risk management process to take place effectively.

Leadership and Commitment

The standard emphasises the importance of a clear commitment to risk management by senior management, including "Ensuring that the necessary resources are allocated to managing risk" (para 5.2). I strongly endorse this sentiment, which is supported by empirical evidence. For instance, Roberts and Stephens (2009) found that the visible engagement of senior management in an exercise programme was strongly associated with the maturity of BCM arrangements within the Medical Research Council.

Integration

This section is really just a statement of principle: "Risk management should be a part of, and not separate from, the organisational purpose, governance, leadership and commitment, strategy, objectives and operations" (para 5.3). As stated previously, the approach to risk management proposed in this book supports this aim by presenting risk management decisions as perfectly normal business decisions, not some special class of judgement requiring its own rules.

Design

This section gives most of the practical detail of the risk management framework, including assigning roles and responsibilities for carrying out risk management, allocating resources and establishing effective processes for communication and consultation. I would absolutely endorse the importance of paying attention to all of these aspects.

Assigning roles and responsibilities goes way beyond identifying individuals at an operational level to carry out specific risk management activities. I have already highlighted the potential for agency problems, including both:

■ Senior managers exploiting their position to invest in risk management that is purely (or primarily) beneficial to themselves; and
■ Senior managers neglecting risk management that would benefit other stakeholders because it does not benefit them personally.

So, robust assurance and governance arrangements are needed, with clear oversight of risk management by the Board. There is in fact some empirical evidence in the academic literature on risk-taking (see sidebar in Chapter 1) that firms where the CEO is more incentivised to take risks are more likely to have more mature risk management programmes, suggesting that company directors are aware of this agency problem and have taken steps to mitigate it.

Para 5.4.4 highlights the need for senior management to "ensure allocation of appropriate resources for risk management". The wording here is subtly different to the "necessary resources" (para 5.2) quoted above, and highlights the importance of constantly reviewing if the current investment in risk management is actually creating value for stakeholders. I will return to this question in Chapters 7 and 8. Finally, regarding communication and consultation. I have repeatedly emphasised the importance of incorporating the perspectives of multiple stakeholder groups (internal and external) into risk management, so it is necessary to design an architecture that allows for a free flow of information in both directions, and gives people confidence that their views have been considered.

Implementation, Evaluation and Improvement

Once again, these sections are largely statements of general principles, such as:

- "Successful implementation of the framework requires the engagement and awareness of stakeholders" (para 5.5);
- "the organisation should periodically measure risk management framework performance against its purpose ... indicators and expected behaviours" (para 5.6); and
- "The organisation should continually monitor and adapt the risk management framework to address external and internal changes" (para 5.7).

I will return in particular to the measurement of the effectiveness of risk management in Chapter 7.

The Risk Management Process

ISO 31000 (2018) outlines a relatively straightforward process for managing risk, consisting of six iterative steps that are undertaken in a coordinated manner, but not necessarily in strict sequence. It is important to note that the risk management process contributes to the design of the risk management framework described above, so the relationship between process and framework is also iterative rather than strictly sequential. The six steps are:

■ Communication and consultation;
■ Scope, context and criteria;
■ Risk assessment;
■ Risk treatment;
■ Monitoring and review; and
■ Recording and reporting.

Risk assessment is further broken down into three sub-processes:

■ Risk identification;
■ Risk analysis; and
■ Risk evaluation

Whilst the process, as outlined, appears quite logical, as discussed at the start of the chapter, the observed results of organisations slavishly following this process have been rather disappointing. In the following sections, I will attempt to identify some of the reasons for this within the individual process steps.

Communication and Consultation

Echoing the stakeholder perspective developed in Chapter 1, para 6.2 states that "Communication and consultation with appropriate external and internal stakeholders should take place within and throughout all steps of the risk management process". The standard proceeds to, quite correctly, emphasise the importance of understanding and accommodating differing stakeholders' views in defining risk criteria, identifying risks and agreeing a treatment plan. In outlining my proposed approach to risk management in Chapters 4-6, I will assume that appropriate plans for communication and consultation have been established.

Scope, Context and Criteria

This is where the closest connection between process and framework is found, and there is considerable overlap between these two sections in the standard. Following the emphasis on the views of internal and external stakeholders in the previous section, the need to establish the "external context" and "internal context" for the risk management process is stressed. The section also includes guidance on establishing risk criteria, which it defines as specifying "the amount and type of risk that [the organisation] may or may not take" (para 6.3.4). I view setting risk criteria as a broader process of understanding and reconciling different stakeholders' risk perspectives: I look in detail at this in Chapter 4. Although ISO 31000 does not use the term, defining risk criteria is sometimes referred to more loosely as establishing the organisation's "risk appetite".

Risk Assessment

The risk analysis stage, comprising the steps of risk identification, risk analysis and risk evaluation, is where I disagree most profoundly with ISO 31000 orthodoxy. Clearly, there is a need to identify risks, and I will discuss some practical approaches to doing this in Chapter 5. However, as one moves into the risk analysis step, there is a real danger of becoming overly

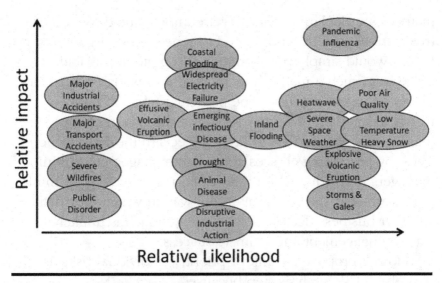

Figure 3.1   A likelihood and impact matrix

focused on the risks themselves, rather than the potential risk treatments.

In Chapter 1, I discussed the idea of risk being a combination of the likelihood of an event occurring and the consequences (to particular stakeholder groups) should the event occur, noting that this idea has ancient origins but is also at the heart of all modern good practice guidance. Unfortunately, the practice of ranking or prioritising the severity of risks, based on multiplying some sort of ratings for likelihood and impact, as part of the risk analysis phase, has become very widespread. This results in the ubiquitous risk matrices that do so much to impede the progress of risk management. Figure 3.1 is based on the UK government's National Risk Register in 2015*.

Other authors (e.g. Hubbard (2020, Chapter 8)) have detailed the many and various technical shortcomings of risk

---

* Previous editions of the UK National Risk Register have now been withdrawn, but the 2020 version is available at https://www.gov.uk/government/publications /national-risk-register-2020.

matrices, particularly when they are implemented in a qualitative manner, and I do not intend to repeat those arguments here. I would simply point out that it is quite impossible to judge from such a matrix how much it is reasonable to spend to try to move a risk from one particular position on the matrix to another. (You may recall the discussion of applying this sort of approach to R&D projects in the Introduction.) Thus, by presenting choices about risk management to senior managers in this manner, one is requiring executives to think in a completely different way to the way in which they make all other business decisions. Such an approach is unlikely to lead to engagement and ultimate success.

I do not propose to rank or prioritise individual risks as part of the risk analysis step because:

■ One is primarily interested in solutions (risk treatments) rather than problems (risks); and
■ One is interested in the impact on stakeholders of the overall portfolio of risks (not the effect of individual risks).

I therefore confine the risk analysis step to estimating distributions for likelihood and impact, and combining these to model distributions of outcomes, the methods for which will be described in detail in Chapter 5.

The final step within the risk assessment stage is risk evaluation. Continuing the focus on individual risks, ISO 31000 (2009, para 5.4.4) states that "The purpose of risk evaluation is to assist in making decisions, based on the outcomes of risk analysis, about which risks need treatment and the priority for treatment implementation". It is unclear how one can make these decisions before even considering what risk treatments may be available (see next section). More fundamentally, in the context of my proposed approach, no individual risk is acceptable or not acceptable to stakeholders on its own, so risk evaluation, in the sense implied by ISO 31000, really has no meaning. I will, instead, move directly to considering potential risk treatments.

Risk Treatment

Having identified a risk, there are basically four approaches that can be taken, often referred to as the "4 T's": *

- Treat (risk reduction);
- Transfer (risk transfer);
- Terminate (risk avoidance); and
- Tolerate (risk acceptance).

These are discussed in more detail below.

Whenever one thinks of managing risk, the most obvious response is *risk reduction*: an intervention to reduce the likelihood of occurrence and/or the impact should the event occur. Interventions could include any of the following:

- Investment in physical security, IT security and other measures (e.g. flood defences, sprinkler systems) to reduce the risk of specific events taking place;
- Staff training and changes in working practices (potentially underpinned by formal management systems) to reduce the likelihood of specific events (e.g. data breaches) taking place;
- Contingency planning to mitigate the effects of disruptions should they occur (e.g. "business continuity management" or "crisis management" planning).

---

* The terminology is somewhat confusing as "risk treatment" is the overarching step in the ISO 31000 risk management process, but the term "treat" is widely used in the practitioner community to denote one specific approach, "risk reduction". I will therefore use the terms "reduction", "transfer", "avoidance" and "acceptance" in order to avoid confusion.

It is important to highlight that, whilst there is often a focus on ways of reducing specific risks, broader contingency planning to deal with the effects of a range of disruptions often offers the best value for money.

Whilst risk reduction is generally the default solution, it is important to keep an open mind: there may be alternative forms of risk treatment that give a greater return on investment. Sometimes it is possible to *transfer* (some part of) the risk to another party. Clearly, this counter-party will require appropriate compensation (directly or indirectly) to accept the additional risk so, generally, this approach actually reduces the expected outcome for the organisation. However, risk transfer may still be attractive to some stakeholder groups if the reduction in the likelihood of extreme losses and/or the reduction in variability of outcomes is sufficient. Historically, risk transfer has generally been achieved by purchasing insurance (see Attitudes to Insurance sidebar), and the insurance market continues to evolve to meet emerging needs with many new offerings in terms of business interruption and cyber policies in recent years.

ATTITUDES TO INSURANCE SIDEBAR

It is often believed or assumed that public sector organisations are inherently more risk averse than their private sector peers. The following example demonstrates that this is not always the case.

I worked some years ago with a public sector organisation which had a policy of only purchasing insurance where there was a legal requirement to do so. Thus, they did not purchase cover for their buildings, equipment or business interruption. Having never come across this approach before it seemed odd at first, but I gradually came to see its value.

As stated above, risk transfer generally *reduces* expected outcomes: one has to pay a third party more than the expected loss in order to induce them to accept the transfer. This leads to the general advice to avoid "pound-swapping", that is where one insures against regular minor losses that the organisation could actually absorb within its normal profit and loss. Rather, the justification for insurance arises solely from the value of reducing the likelihood of catastrophic losses. At the corporate level, the organisation in question judged that:

■ The likelihood of a catastrophic loss was inherently low; and
■ The likelihood could further be reduced by cost-effective risk reduction.*

Hence, there was no strong justification for the discretionary purchase of insurance.

I cannot say if all stakeholder groups had been consulted on this approach (for instance, staff may have preferred the reassurance of having an insurance policy in place), but it certainly had a very positive effect in focusing members of senior management on risk reduction. It was also of great value in persuading individual business unit leaders to take risk management seriously: absent an insurance payout, there was no certainty that buildings or equipment would be replaced on a like-for-like basis. Thus, following a disruption, the Board might choose to restore the affected business unit(s) to their pre-disaster position,

---

* It can be argued that there was also the expectation that the UK government would provide emergency financial support if this was ever required. This may be true, but is no different to a private firm expecting that its owners would commit more money if required in a crisis, so long as it fundamentally remains viable.

or, they might decide instead to invest in completely new areas of activity that promised better returns on investment in the future.

Increasingly though, insurance solutions face competition from the capital markets. In addition to well-established derivatives markets to manage foreign exchange, commodity price and credit risks, there are now innovative products such as catastrophe bonds and weather derivatives to mitigate the (financial) impact of operational disruptions (see Alternative Risk Transfer sidebar). Risk can also, in some cases, be transferred to customers or suppliers through contractual arrangements.

ALTERNATIVE RISK TRANSFER SIDEBAR

Harnessing the huge capacity of the global capital markets, a vast range of alternative risk transfer (ART) products has emerged in recent years, to complement the established (and evolving) insurance market. One form of ART is novel forms of debt financing. "Forgivable bonds" are issued on the basis that the principal and/or interest is forgiven if a defined event occurs. The trigger can be a defined move in commodity prices or exchange rates, or a specific event, such as a natural disaster or terrorist incident. The latter are known as "catastrophe bonds" or just "cat bonds". For instance, the 2006 World Cup was partly financed by a $260 million cat bond with the trigger for forgiving the debt being a terrorist incident. Cat bond placements in 2020 ranged in size from $3.75 million to $700 million, and covered risks including earthquakes, storms, flooding, wildfires and volcanoes. The use of cat bonds is certainly not limited to the corporate sector; in an interesting development in 2021, the Danish Red Cross (and partners) placed a $3 million bond to provide aid in response to certain specified volcanic eruptions. Obviously, investors require higher yield for these novel forms of debt, but cat bonds have proven attractive because the risk of having to forgive the debt is not generally correlated with the overall risk of bad debt in the economy.

Another whole family of ART solutions are based on derivatives. These products have the advantage of reducing the "moral hazard" associated with insurance: payouts are based on external indices as a proxy for losses, so purchasers remain incentivised to continue to mitigate their own risk in other ways. Obviously, the market in credit, interest rate and foreign exchange derivatives provide a mechanism to transfer a wide range of financial risks; but there are also derivative-based products for transferring operational risks. Perhaps the most well established of these products are weather derivatives, which are widely used by energy firms. The value of the derivative is based on an appropriate weather index, such as average temperature or monthly rainfall in a certain geographic region. An energy firm can thus hedge its risk of reduced revenues due to a warm winter by buying weather derivatives whose value increases with the average temperature in January. There are also derivatives, linked to specific adverse events: "catastrophe options". The value of these is linked to a "catastrophe index", typically based on property losses from weather or natural disasters in a particular region. Catastrophe options are principally used by insurance firms to reinsure their potential losses.

Early on in my career in risk management, I attempted (unsuccessfully) to pioneer another form of ART: a "contingent line of credit". I had noticed, in the practice of business continuity management, how little attention was paid to financing recovery after a disruption. There was often an assumption that insurance claims would cover any costs but, even when this is so, there may be a significant delay in payments. Thus, following Hurricane Katrina, many US businesses were only saved by loans administered by the US Small Business Administration, and, following a range of flooding events in the United Kingdom, many small businesses were saved by loans administered by the Federation of Small Businesses. Likewise, during Covid-19, tens of thousands of firms in the United Kingdom were kept alive through an unprecedented combination of government grants and loans. Whilst these schemes have been invaluable, they all suffer from the drawback of a lack of certainty: firms have no knowledge in advance of an incident what support will be available, and on what terms, so have no solid basis upon which to make recovery plans.

My proposed solution was a contingent line of credit or "continuity bond". The idea was that, unlike a normal line of credit, where the borrower can draw on the facility at any time, with a continuity bond, borrowers could only use the facility in the event of one of a range of specified operational disruptions (e.g. fire, flood). Thus, the organisation could plan their recovery from disruption in the certain knowledge of having access to an agreed sum of money, on agreed terms, in the immediate aftermath of the disruption, but the lender was managing their risk (compared to extending a conventional line of credit) as the borrower could not just draw on the loan whenever they wished. However, when I first pitched the idea to one of our major banks in the benign lending environment that existed in 2005, they said that there was no need for such a product as "If one of our customers needed a line of credit in an emergency, we would just extend it to them – no problem". When I tried again (with a different major bank) only four years later, lending practices had gone to the other extreme, and my idea was dismissed as "far too risky". So, at the time of writing, it remains just an idea.

Risk avoidance represents a third alternative, which is often overlooked. Risk avoidance means that the organisation simply ceases or adapts a particular activity, or activities, to change the overall loss distribution. Examples of risk avoidance could include, discontinuing particular product lines, ceasing operations in specific countries or modifying operating hours.

Having reviewed all the potential risk treatments, including avoidance, related to a particular risk, it may be concluded that there is no business case to implement any of these. Conventionally, the organisation is then said to have decided to *accept* that risk. However, in the approach outlined in the following chapters, the focus is on whether stakeholders can tolerate the overall loss distribution, rather than individual risks, so the concept of accepting one specific risk is not really meaningful.

Monitoring and Review

A systematic process of monitoring and review is absolutely critical for two reasons:

- ■ To measure the effectiveness of current risk management activities; and
- ■ To enable continuous improvement.

I will return to the first point in considerable detail in Chapter 7. Monitoring and review is another critical point at which the risk management process interacts with the risk management framework, where responsibilities for monitoring and reviewing activities must be clearly defined.

Recording and Reporting

It is crucial that the whole risk management process is auditable, and is robust against turnover of staff. It is therefore necessary to properly document how the process is implemented. This will be particularly important for the quantitative approach to risk management outlined in Chapters 4-6. Emphasising, once again, the importance of stakeholders (internal and external), it is also essential that information on the outcomes of risk management activities is shared effectively, in order to inform an ongoing discussion of scope, context and criteria. As stated in the previous discussion about communication and consultation, it will be assumed in the following chapters that appropriate mechanisms to share this information are in place.

Risk Displacement and Risk Compensation

One of the stated objectives of this book is to refocus attention on risk treatment. In concluding this chapter, I should therefore like to return briefly to the risk treatment step in the risk management process in order to highlight a couple of potential pitfalls.

When undertaking risk treatment, it is always important to bear in mind that the measures that are taken to mitigate risks may not have the desired effect. Indeed, many academics and practitioners argue that one never truly gets rid of risk, one simply moves or transforms it; this is known as *risk displacement*. Risk displacement can be particularly problematic as it tends to create new risks which are less visible and less well understood. Discussing this phenomenon in the context of security management, Schneier (2003, p.14) proposes the following checklist of questions to go through before taking any action:

- What assets are you trying to protect?
- What are the risks to those assets?
- How well does the security solution mitigate those risks?
- What other risks does the security solution cause?
- What costs and trade-offs does the security solutions impose?

I like to illustrate the use of the checklist with the example of the response by train operating companies to a spate of bombs at railway stations around London in 1993. The bombs tended to be hidden in the litter bins at stations, so operators responded by removing all bins. This, superficially attractive, solution had two significant drawbacks, which would have been immediately highlighted by Schneier's checklist:

- The security solution proposed was only a very partial mitigation of the identified risks to the assets (passengers) as there were many other places to hide a device; and
- The removal of bins led to a significant increase in the amount of littering at stations, creating a greater risk of fire and infestation and impacting negatively on the whole travel experience.

Sadly, having been removed, it was a long time before the litter bins were replaced, so the negative effects of this ill-considered solution persisted long after the terrorist threat receded. If one simply substitutes "risk treatment" for "security solution", the checklist can be applied much more generally.

The outcomes of risk treatment may also not be as expected (hoped) because of *risk compensation*. Adams

(1995, p.14)) argues that we each have an inherent tolerance of risk (he likens it to a setting on a thermostat) so that, as our environment becomes (or even just appears to become) less risky, we choose to take on more risk. Thus, the rate at which motorcyclists were being killed actually increased immediately after the wearing of crash helmets became compulsory in the United Kingdom in 1973. Whilst the risk of serious head injuries was significantly reduced, people (in aggregate) responded to the feeling of reduced vulnerability by riding less carefully, and fatal injuries through other means (e.g. crush injuries to the chest) rose as a result. In an organisational context this may mean that people respond to improvements in formal risk management by being less careful in their day-to-day work.

We cannot therefore assume that the outcomes of risk treatment will be as intended; hence, once again, the critical need for effective monitoring and review.

Summary

Integrated risk management aims to create value by managing the whole portfolio of risks to which an organisation is exposed in a consistent manner. However, empirical studies of the implementation of specific risk management approaches, such as enterprise risk management and business continuity management, suggest that this consistency is not easy to achieve in practice.

ISO 31000 provides detailed guidance on the implementation of integrated risk management, consisting primarily of a risk management framework and a risk management process.

I have argued that the risk management process described in ISO 31000, specifically the risk assessment stage, leads to a focus on risks rather than risk management; it also tends to lead towards consideration of risks in isolation. The modified approach, which is described in the next three chapters, aims to address these criticisms.

Risk treatments may not have the desired effect because of risk displacement and/or risk compensation.

References

Adams J, 1995, *Risk*, London: Routledge.

Arena M, Arnaboldi M and Azzone G, 2010, The Organizational Dynamics of Enterprise Risk Management, *Accounting, Organizations and Society*, 35: 659–675.

COSO, 2004, *Enterprise Risk Management*, Committee of Sponsoring Organisations of the Treadway Commission.

Green C, 2006, You Can't Manage What You Can't Measure: Benchmarking Business Continuity, *The Business Continuity Journal*, 1(1): 9–20.

Hubbard D, 2020, *The Failure of Risk Management: Why it's Broken and How to Fix It*, 2nd Edition, Hoboken, NJ: Wiley.

ISO, 2009, *ISO 31000 Risk Management - Guidance and Best Practice*, Geneva: International Organization for Standardization.

ISO, 2018, *ISO 31000 Risk Management - Guidance and Best Practice*, Geneva: International Organization for Standardization.

Leitch M, 2010, ISO 31000:2009 – The New International Standard on Risk Management, *Risk Analysis*, 30(6): 887–892.

Merton R, 2005, You Have More Capital Than You Think, *Harvard Business Review*, November 2005: 84–94.

Power M, 2007, *Organized Uncertainty: Designing a World of Risk Management*, Oxford: Oxford University Press.

Roberts P and Stephens M, 2009, Implementing Business Continuity Management in a Distributed Organisation, *The Business Continuity Journal*, 3(4): 16–26.

Schneier B, 2003, *Beyond Fear: Thinking Sensibly about Security in an Uncertain World*, New York, NY: Copernicus Books.

Chapter 4

Scope, Context and Criteria

Building on the discussion of integrated risk management, and ISO 31000 in particular, in the previous chapter, this chapter begins to describe a proposed approach to better risk management. In this chapter, I will focus on the scope, context and criteria of risk management, before proceeding to look at risk assessment in Chapter 5 and risk treatment in Chapter 6. To reiterate once again, the overall aim of this approach is to be able to present proposals for investing in risk management to senior managers as normal business decisions, based on robust estimates of the return on investment. As discussed in the previous chapter, there is considerable overlap in ISO 31000 between this process step and elements of the risk management framework.

I have already discussed the risk perspectives of different stakeholder groups in some detail in Chapters 1 and 2, and the need to engage with internal and external stakeholders was repeatedly emphasised in ISO 31000. A good understanding of the organisation's stakeholder groups and their risk perspectives

DOI: 10.4324/9781003225157-4

forms the context for any risk management programme. To summarise some of the key stakeholders' perspectives:

- Owners (where these exist) will be primarily concerned with expected outcomes, the variability in outcomes and the likelihood and cost of financial distress;
- Senior managers will be primarily concerned with missing targets; and
- Other staff members, customers, suppliers and lenders will primarily be concerned with the likelihood of financial distress.

This chapter begins by looking at how these different shareholder perspectives can be used in setting the organisation's risk criteria. The aim of integrated risk management is that these risk criteria are then consistently applied to all risks but, as will be discussed, this is not always the case in practice. Ensuring consistency involves various elements of the risk management framework, most importantly the assigning of roles, authorities, responsibilities and accountabilities, as well as appropriate arrangements for monitoring and review. The chapter concludes by discussing how one justifies the resources to be allocated to risk management.

Agreeing Risk Criteria

Consideration of stakeholders' risk perspectives should enable the organisation to express its risk criteria, that is, what sort of risks are acceptable or tolerable to stakeholders. Logically, stakeholders will only wish to accept risks if there is expected to be some benefit to them, so what one is really trying to establish is answers to questions such as:

- How much compensation do stakeholders require to accept an increased probability of an extreme event; and

- How much compensation do stakeholders require to accept an increased variability in outcomes?

However, in keeping with the focus on risk treatments rather than risks themselves, these two key risk criteria can be more usefully phrased as:

- How much are stakeholders willing to pay to reduce the probability of an extreme event; and
- How much are stakeholders willing to pay to reduce variability in outcomes?

In order to implement a quantitative approach to managing risk, as advocated in this book, one actually needs to put a figure on these values, rather than a vague statement of intent or a list of principles. As has been discussed previously though, this may require the reconciling of very different risk perspectives of different stakeholder groups, so agreeing on these risk criteria represents the first real challenge to a quantitative approach. Recalling the discussion of reconciling conflicting interests in Chapter 1, expressing risk criteria numerically will likely involve elements of satisficing rather than optimising, and the values may well evolve with time and experience. However, as I argue time and again throughout this book, it is preferable to have an initial estimate that people can then argue about and improve over time, rather than conceal these tensions under vague, qualitative verbiage.

The potential for conflicts of interest also highlights, once again, the criticality of establishing a sound risk management framework. Roles and responsibilities, up to Board level, need to be clearly defined, and lines of communication, internal and external, established to ensure that different stakeholders' views are heard and incorporated into the risk criteria. Critically, the risk management framework needs to be robust enough to ensure that no single stakeholder group (e.g. senior

management) can appropriate the risk management programme for their own benefit.

Reducing the Probability of an Extreme Event

In considering extreme events, at a very minimum it is necessary to calculate how much it is reasonable to spend to reduce
the probability of a loss that would result in bankruptcy. There
may also be other levels of extreme loss short of this that need
consideration in their own right. For instance, any loss that
was large enough to breach banking covenants, or to violate
conditions imposed by a regulator, would have a significant
impact on the organisation. Indeed, Hubbard (2020, p.69)
proposes plotting a complete "loss exceedance curve", illustrat-
ing the acceptable probability of any level of loss. Particularly
within the public and not-for-profit sectors, there may also be
significant value in reducing the likelihood of non-financial
extreme events that could, for example, damage the organisation's reputation or put it in breach of its contractual or statutory obligations.

Focusing solely on the probability of bankruptcy, a number of stakeholder groups will be impacted by such an event,
including:

- Owners who see the value of their investment wiped out;
- Lenders, particularly unsecured lenders, whose loans are
  not (fully) repaid;
- Staff who suffer personal financial loss; and
- Customers and suppliers who face disruption to their sup-
  ply chain.

Of these, the cost to owners (where applicable) and the cost
to lenders are relatively easy to calculate. Considering the
example of a small firm with £600,000 of shareholders' equity,

total losses of greater than £600,000 would result in bankruptcy and the loss of all of this equity. If one can reduce the annual likelihood of a loss of over £600,000 by 1%, then the expected loss to owners has been reduced by £6,000 a year (1% of £600,000). If, in addition, the organisation has loans of £1 million, and lenders expect to be able to recover only 50% of this amount in the event of bankruptcy, then this reduction in the likelihood of financial distress would save an additional £5,000 (1% of 50% of £1 million) annually.* Thus, as a starting point, one can say that for this firm it is worth paying at least £11,000/year for a 1% reduction in the likelihood of sustaining a loss of greater than £600,000. Expert judgement can then be applied to evaluate the impacts on other stakeholder groups in order to estimate the overall benefit of reducing the probability of bankruptcy.

Reducing Variability of Outcomes

Chapters 1 and 2 explored a range of reasons why owners would wish to minimise variability in performance. As well as the practical benefits of maintaining stable performance, such as minimising taxes and adjustment costs, I introduced the argument that variability is inherently undesirable to owners. It was clear from those discussions that attitudes towards variability in outcomes will depend entirely on the nature of ownership. I will look here at attitudes towards variability of outcomes under three specific types of ownership: entrepreneurial firms, corporations and public sector/not-for-profit organisations.

In the context of an entrepreneurial firm with a single owner, one can directly apply Utility Theory (or a more

---

* Lenders' expectations of the probability of default and loss given default will be directly passed on in the cost of the loan.

modern approach to individual choice such as Prospect Theory) to estimate the value of a reduction in the variability of outcomes. Attempting this in the rarefied environment of an MBA workshop, where students were asked to role-play being an entrepreneur with all their wealth tied up in a business similar to the one described in the previous section, I found that, for instance, a reduction in the standard deviation of profit and loss from £100,000 to £50,000 was valued at about £20,000.* However, the empirical evidence reviewed in Chapter 2 shows that the level of compensation required to accept variability in outcomes is very dependent on the prevailing economic conditions. Therefore, an alternative way to estimate this risk criterion, based on inferring stakeholders' risk perspectives from a profit and loss model for the organisation, will be developed in Chapter 6. This yields a relationship between expected returns and variability of returns, specific to that organisation at that particular point in time, that is, presumably, acceptable to all stakeholder groups.

As discussed previously, investors in large corporations can significantly reduce the risk to themselves of variations in performance of individual firms simply by diversifying their portfolios. Thus, one would expect the value to well-diversified investors of specific risk treatments to be significantly less than their value to entrepreneurial owners. It is possible to gain a good idea of the value to such investors of reducing variability from empirical studies of stock market data. Malkiel and Xu (1997), studying publicly traded US firms from 1963 to 1990, and Dempsey et al. (2001), studying publicly traded Australian firms from 1990 to 2000, found very similar results. In both cases, it appears that stock market investors require roughly a 1% increase in annual returns for each 4% increase in the idiosyncratic variability of returns (i.e. variability not correlated

---

* It is interesting to note that, even in this reasonably homogeneous group, there were considerable differences in the perceived value of reducing variability.

with the market). Once again though, this will presumably depend on economic conditions.

As regards public sector and not-for-profit organisations, there is no ownership argument, but there may still be practical reasons for wishing to minimise variability. Absent a theoretical model or empirical evidence, it is recommended to follow the bootstrapping approach, described in Chapter 6, to infer the value to the organisation's stakeholders of reducing variability.

Ownership and Delegated Authority

An effective integrated risk management system requires ownership of risks at an appropriate level throughout the organisation; this involves individual managers making risk-based decisions within their own areas of responsibility. However, in making these decisions managers should consistently apply the corporate risk criteria, not one appropriate to their own business unit or department.

I have previously noted that risk-taking decisions should be based on exactly the same criteria as risk management decisions. Thaler (2015, p.187) eloquently illustrates the problem of applying inappropriate risk criteria in the context of risk-taking, in a story about running a workshop for a group of executives working for a large print media company. Each of the 23 executives in the workshop was asked if they would accept an opportunity for their own business unit that offered a 50% chance of $1 million gain and a 50% chance of $500,000 loss. Although the expected outcome was positive, only 3 of the 23 executives taking part said that they would accept the project, but their CEO, who was observing the workshop, wanted them all to proceed with the projects. Why were the decisions made by almost all of the executives not in line with their CEO's wishes?

It would appear that the majority of the executives were applying inappropriate risk criteria based on the perspective of their own business unit and, potentially, their own self-interest. As I discussed in Chapter 1, managers are generally concerned with the likelihood of missing targets: a loss of $500,000 would probably be very significant for most of the business units as stand-alone entities and would most likely result in a missed target (and lost bonus). However, the business units are not stand-alone entities, and if all 23 executives had opted to take the opportunity, there is a very significant potential upside, and less than a 5% chance of the firm losing any money.* This example echoes my initial comments about how integrated risk management seeks to manage risks as a portfolio.

Rabin and Bazerman (2019) provide a detailed and entertaining critique of organisational decision-making, which further highlights the need for a consistent application of risk criteria across the organisation. Whilst the main focus of the article is on the observed tendency towards risk aversion, the authors also highlight the problem of inconsistent risk attitudes across an organisation: typically, some functions within the organisation (e.g. sales) are positively risk-seeking, whilst others (e.g. legal) are very risk-averse. Rather than these differing approaches to risk balancing each other out, as one might imagine, the waste of resources through unnecessarily risk-averse decisions in some parts of the organisation means that there is less available in reserves to deal with the consequences of risk-seeking decisions made elsewhere in the organisation. Thus, inconsistency in the application of risk criteria actually makes the organisation *more* vulnerable.

---

* In order for the firm to make a loss, at least 16 of the 23 projects would need to make a loss (16 losses of $500,000 and 7 gains of $1 million equals an overall loss of $1 million). The probability of at least 16 losses out of 23 in a 50/50 bet, such as this is 4.7%.

Justifying Resources

ISO 31000 (2009, para 5.3.4) emphasises that "The management of risk should be undertaken with full consideration of the need to justify the resources used in carrying out risk management". In Chapter 6, I will show how potential risk treatments can be evaluated based on a straightforward return on investment calculation, so there is no need to provide further justification for the resources committed to individual risk treatments. However, this does not justify the central costs of running a risk management programme; these will normally consist primarily of staff costs, but may also include for example consultancy fees, IT equipment and software licences. There is no elegant solution to this problem, but I can offer some practical advice. First and foremost, my professional experience is that these central costs are dwarfed by the costs of mitigating specific risks: typically, central costs would be an order of magnitude less than implementation costs. That is not to say that they can be ignored though. I would strongly advocate an incremental approach to implementing risk management, perhaps using consultants and contractors initially before recruiting an in-house team, and measuring the return on investment at each stage before expanding the programme. I will return to this issue in Chapter 7, when I look at measuring the effectiveness of risk management, and, once again, in Chapter 8.

Summary

In this chapter I have begun to outline a quantitative approach to risk management, broadly based on the principles of integrated risk management outlined in ISO 31000. In particular, I have reinforced the need for an effective risk management framework and discussed the scope, context and criteria of risk management.

It is vital to agree on appropriate risk criteria; this requires effective, two-way communication with all stakeholder groups. I looked specifically at the value (to stakeholders) of reducing the likelihood of an extreme loss and reducing the variability in outcomes. The importance of ensuring that managers throughout the organisation apply the agreed risk criteria consistently was also highlighted.

The resources committed to risk management must be justified. It was suggested that a flexible, incremental approach to implementation allows an organisation to gradually build up the data required to justify further expenditure as the programme rolls out.

References

Dempsey M, Drew M and Veeraraghavan M, 2001, *Idiosyncratic Risk and Australian Equity Returns*, Queensland University of Technology, School of Economics and Finance, available at https://core.ac.uk/download/pdf/6524176.pdf (downloaded 26th Feb 2021).

Hubbard D, 2020, *The Failure of Risk Management: Why it's Broken and How to Fix It*, 2nd Edition, Hoboken, NJ: Wiley.

ISO, 2009, *ISO 31000 Risk Management - Guidance and Best Practice*, International Organization for Standardization.

Malkiel B and Xu Y, 1997, Idiosyncratic Risk and Security Returns, *Journal of Portfolio Management*, 23: 9–14.

Rabin M and Bazerman M, 2019, Fretting about Modest Risks is a Mistake, *California Management Review*, 61(3): 34–48.

Thaler R, 2015, *Misbehaving: The Making of Behavioural Economics*, London: Allen Lane.

Chapter 5

Risk Assessment

As described in Chapter 3, risk assessment is conventionally broken down into the three steps of risk identification, risk analysis and risk evaluation. It was argued that risk evaluation was meaningless in the context of the approach proposed here; detailed guidance for the remaining two steps is presented below. Of necessity, this approach is quantitative and the process will be illustrated with a simple numerical example. The numerical example is based on a small entrepreneurial firm, but an alternative example, specifically applicable to the public and not-for-profit sectors, is provided in Annex C.

I appreciate that some readers may find mathematics off-putting, but it should be stressed that the whole purpose is to illustrate concepts in risk management, not to improve the readers' knowledge of statistical techniques! Ultimately, there is no need for the person overseeing a risk management programme to understand in detail the statistical techniques that are used; individuals with the required data analysis skills may already be available within your organisation and, if not, they can increasingly be found externally.

Risk Identification

Identifying hazards to an organisation is comparatively easy; as humans we seem to be very adept at this. There are also lots of publicly available sources of risk information: from high-profile news stories of disasters through to specialised information from government agencies, regulators, trade organisations and professional bodies. Some useful sources of risk information are listed at Annex D. In practice, much useful risk information about the organisation can be gained simply by talking to a suitably wide range of staff members about incidents, near-misses and other issues that concern them: people are generally very happy to talk unless a specific risk may be seen to reflect negatively on themselves. At the risk of stating the obvious, it is important to acknowledge that the list of risks will always be incomplete. However, as with all other aspects of my proposed approach, the aim is to incrementally improve over time. Below I discuss three important considerations for the risk identification process: what level of granularity of risks to capture, how to categorise risks and what information to record and report as part of this step in the process.

Granularity of Risks

A key question that always crops up when identifying risks is what level of granularity to capture risks at. In some sense there is no right answer to this but, at least in the field of operational risk where most of my experience lies, I would recommend focusing on the business impact rather than the specific cause. For example, denial of access to your building may occur for many different reasons (flooding, gas leak, police cordon, fire at neighbouring premises) but the business impact is essentially the same. Also, whilst it may be worth considering specific risk mitigations for some of these causes (e.g. flooding), most of the causes are largely out of your control, so the primary risk treatment is going to be contingency planning for continuing critical business activities for a period of time without your building. Likewise, staff may be unavailable for a number of reasons (industrial action, epidemic/pandemic, severe weather), but the business impact and many of the likely risk treatments are the same. For all these reasons, and for the sake of clarity, it often makes sense to aggregate risks in this way.

In offering this general advice, it is necessary to highlight one technical, but very important, point. Any statistical techniques applied to loss distributions are based on the data, all being drawn from the same "population". Following the advice given above you might, for instance, combine all outages of a particular critical IT system to form a single distribution of duration of outages. However, this could include both hardware and software events, with very different characteristics.* Any statistical analysis of this distribution will therefore be systematically flawed. Rather than deal with this at the stage of risk identification though, it is recommended to proceed on the basis outlined above, but to be very mindful at the risk analysis stage (see below) of any signs of erroneously merging different populations.

The question of granularity is also linked to the discussion in Chapter 2 about the particular difficulties of dealing with catastrophic incidents/crises/black-swan events. By definition, a black-swan event cannot be foreseen in advance, and there is a practical limit to how many different scenarios can be included in any analysis. Once again, this problem can be

---

* This is not laziness; we may not know in advance if different types of events have different characteristics. If the duration of outages is dominated by, for example, call-out time for specialist IT support and the time taken to restore and validate data following a disruption, outages with different root causes may actually have very similar distributions of duration.

partially mitigated by focusing on impacts rather than causes. Returning to the example of denial of access to premises, I listed above some routine reasons that this might occur. Other more catastrophic events, such as a terrorist attack or an earthquake, may also result in denial of access. Such events will hardly affect the likelihood of denial of access, but will significantly affect the distribution of impacts: we look at this issue later on in the chapter in the section on risk analysis. As discussed in the previous paragraph, a decision must be made at that stage if there is a requirement to disaggregate any risks.

Risk Categorisations

I talked briefly in Chapter 1 about risk categorisations, and introduced the generic PESTEL/7S's risk categorisation. There are also a number of more detailed industry-specific categorisations: two examples are shown in the sidebar.

INDUSTRY-SPECIFIC RISK CATEGORISATIONS SIDEBAR

Basel II and Basel III (see the discussion on "Trends in Risk Management" in the Introduction) identified the following categories of "Operational Risk Event Types". Whilst the list is developed from a financial services perspective, they are all applicable more widely.

- Internal fraud;
- External fraud;
- Employment practices and workplace safety;
- Clients, products and business practices;
- Damage to physical assets;

■ Business disruption and system failures;
■ Execution, delivery and process management;

Research into risk management in the UK NHS (Okoroh et al., 2002), identified the following categories of risk in the healthcare sector. Whilst some of these risks are industry-specific, others apply across sectors.

■ Customer care;
■ Business transfer risks;
■ Legal risks;
■ Facility transmitted risks;
■ Corporate risks;
■ Commercial risks;
■ Financial and economic risks;

Risk categorisations such as these are very useful during the risk identification process for grouping and organising risks as they emerge, be that through a formal process of analysis or simply brainstorming with a group of staff. Grouping risks in a logical manner such as this then aids the search to identify additional, related risks through further analysis or more brainstorming.

As mentioned above, much useful hazard information can be derived simply from talking to people, but people are often reluctant to talk about risks that may reflect badly on themselves or their organisation. The following risk categorisation, adapted from Elliott, Swartz and Herbane (2002), is therefore highly recommended as it explicitly forces people to think about the internally generated risks (on the left-hand side) that they may feel least comfortable to highlight (Figure 5.1).

However, looking ahead to risk analysis and risk treatment, I would emphasise once again that the most important

Figure 5.1   Categorisation of risks

distinction is between value-adding and passive risks (Merton, 2005). Within the domain of passive risks, upon which we focus, it is often useful to further sub-divide these into "operational" and "financial" risks.

Recording and Reporting

The importance of "Recording and Reporting" as part of the risk management process was highlighted in Chapter 3. Recording and reporting some key information is an integral part of the risk identification stage of the process. This information should include:

■ Who has been interviewed about risks (both internally and externally);
■ What publicly available or paid-for sources of risk information have been accessed; and

■ What criteria have been applied for excluding risks (if applicable).

These details are essential in order to provide confidence to stakeholders in the process, to ensure the continuity of the programme, regardless of any turnover of staff, and to enable continuous improvement.

Risk Analysis

As discussed previously, risk is usually conceptualised as the combination of likelihood (or frequency) of an event and the impact if it occurs: Rather than placing a single number (or, worse still, a meaningless verbal descriptor) on the likelihood and impact of a risk, I would strongly advocate the use of modelled distributions. In this section, I look specifically at modelling two different types of distributions: distributions based on discrete events, and distributions based on continuous variation. I then look at aggregating distributions and conclude by discussing what information to record and report.

Distributions Based on Events

Many operational risks manifest themselves as discrete events (such as fires, floods or IT outages) incurring a loss. Returning to our discussion in Chapter 1 on the definition of risk, one is concerned here solely with negative outcomes. One may therefore refer to the distribution of outcomes as a loss distribution. I will briefly describe below how to model likelihood and impact separately and then combine them to form a loss distribution.

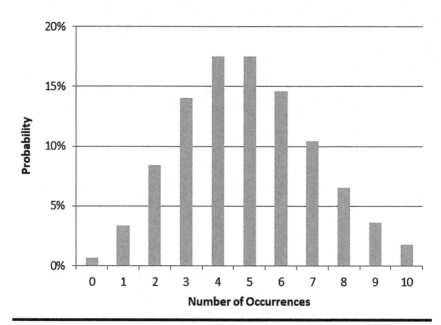

Figure 5.2   Poisson distribution of annual number of IT outages

Frequency Distributions

A simple and useful example of a frequency distribution, the Poisson Distribution, is shown in Figure 5.2. In this example, the number of outages that a particular, business-critical, IT system experiences annually has been modelled. This could be based on some years of historical data, or expert judgement. Obviously, if more data were available, either from within the organisation or external sources, one could estimate with greater confidence: as I have emphasised before, the key to risk management is collecting and analysing the right data. But I would argue that it is always better to begin modelling with a reasonable estimate[*] based on whatever data you have; at the very least this should focus attention on searching for more data going forwards.

---

[*] Hubbard (2020) gives some excellent, detailed guidance on good practice in estimation.

The distribution clearly captures the fact that, whilst the average is five outages per year, having exactly five outages in a year is actually a relatively unlikely outcome (only 17.5% of the time); experiencing two or fewer outages (12.5%) or eight or more outages in any given year (11.9%) are almost as likely.

Impact Distributions

The next step in risk analysis is to derive a distribution of the duration of outages. Once again, this may be based on expert estimates, internal data collected over time or external sources (e.g. publicly available surveys). The Duration of Outages sidebar provides a real example.

DURATION OF OUTAGES SIDEBAR

The London Ambulance Service (LAS) suffered a high-profile outage of their computer-aided dispatch (CAD) system on New Year's Day 2017. The CAD system was offline for approximately 90 minutes, during one of the busiest periods in the year for LAS. LAS managed the impact using their pre-prepared contingency plans, involving both:

- Use of a paper-based dispatch system; and
- Diverting calls to other ambulance services.

The publicly available post-incident report (LAS (2017)) highlighted that there had been ten other outages of the CAD system in the previous three years. The duration of outages varied between 28 minutes and nearly 7 hours. In common with many examples of operational disruptions,

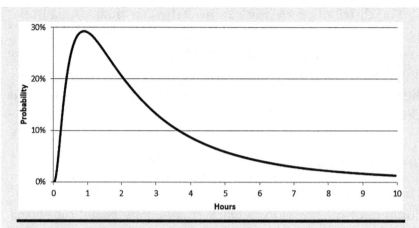

Figure 5.3   Modelled lognormal distribution of duration of CAD outages

the distribution of the duration of these outages was highly "skewed", with a small number of very prolonged outages. There are a number of different statistical distributions that capture this asymmetry, but a straightforward and very useful one is the "lognormal" distribution.

Fitting the data from the LAS post-incident report to a lognormal curve gives the distribution of the duration of CAD outages as shown in Figure 5.3. Thus, while the most likely duration is about one hour, and the median outage is only 2¼ hours, there is:

■ A 10% chance of an outage lasting more than 7½ hours; and
■ A 5% chance of an outage lasting more than 10½ hours.

It is then normally desirable to convert this distribution of durations into a distribution of the financial impacts (e.g. lost profits from missed sales, cash costs of alternative arrangements) from such IT outages; once again, some expert

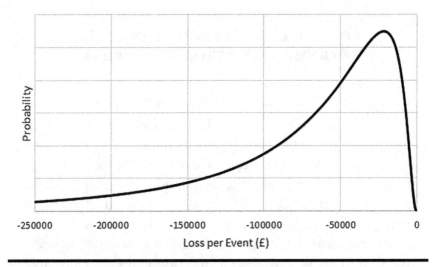

Figure 5.4   Lognormal distribution of losses from an IT outage

judgement may be required in making this conversion. An example of a lognormal distribution of financial impacts is shown in Figure 5.4.*

The lognormal distribution illustrated above captures some important general characteristics observed from studying the impacts of real operational disruptions (e.g. IT outages, cyberattacks and supply chain disruptions). Critically it shows that whilst most incidents have relatively low impacts, there is a small, but non-zero, probability of occasional extremely high impacts. However, there is a considerable body of empirical evidence indicating that some loss distributions have a greater likelihood of extreme losses than is captured by the lognormal. The Power-Law Distribution and Extreme Value Theory sidebar discusses two alternative loss distributions that capture this increased likelihood of extreme losses.

---

* Probability values are not shown as the vertical scale peaks at around 0.00001 (or 0.001%).

POWER-LAW DISTRIBUTION AND EXTREME VALUE THEORY SIDEBAR

Power-law distributions are a simple and intuitive way of modelling phenomena where the likelihood of extreme events is greater than that which is captured by a log-normal curve. The most famous example of a power-law distribution is the magnitude of earthquakes: for each step up on the Richter Scale, the magnitude of an earthquake increases by a factor of 10 and the likelihood of such an earthquake is reduced by a factor of 10. However, good fits of empirical data to power-law distributions have been reported in areas as diverse as the population of cities and number of hits on websites to the intensity of solar flares (Taleb (2007, p.264)). Within the sphere of risk management, power-law distributions have been fitted to impact data for hazards such as movements in financial markets, terrorist attacks and electrical blackouts.

Extreme value theory (EVT) (see Cruz (2002, Chapter 4) for a good introduction) is an umbrella term for a number of mathematical techniques that have specifically been developed to tackle the problem of modelling the extremes of distributions. Originally developed in fields such as engineering and insurance, EVT techniques are now applied very widely in operational risk management within the financial services sector. In recent years, they have also been utilised to model phenomena such as flooding, wild fires and the impact of terrorist attacks.

Whatever distribution is most appropriate, the shape of the "tail" of the distribution is going to have a profound effect on important components of risk, such as the probability of an extreme loss, but this tail has to be estimated on the basis of very limited data. Wherever possible, one should aim to maximise the amount of data available to estimate the tail by using publicly available datasets, or pooling information with peer organisations. Much work has taken place on pooling data and using external data in the context of operational risk management within the financial services sector: Cope (2010) and Dahen and Dionne (2010) are useful references in this regard. It is also important to bear in mind that, in many cases, there is a natural limit to the extent of any loss; for instance, in the case of a data breach, you can only compromise as many customer records as you have customers. In these cases, a truncated distribution is required, which has a zero probability of losses exceeding this natural limit.

Monte-Carlo Modelling

The final stage of the risk analysis process for this sort of operational risk is then to combine these two distributions using a technique known as *Monte-Carlo modelling*. In principle, this involves simulating many (thousands or tens of thousands) possible total losses for a year as follows:

- Randomly draw a possible number of disruptions for that year from the likelihood distribution;
- For each of these disruptions, draw a random value from the impact distribution; and
- Add up all of these impacts to give the total losses for that year.

Then one simply repeats the process the desired number of times. So, for example, using the probability and impact distributions described above might produce the results shown in Table 5.1.

An example of loss distribution based on 1,000 iterations is shown in Figure 5.5 (10,000 iterations would produce a somewhat smoother output but at the cost of greater computational time)

Table 5.1 Illustration of Monte-Carlo Simulation

Iteration	Annual Losses	Loss 1	Loss 2	Loss 3	Loss 4	Loss 5	Total Loss
1	2	£15,000	£100,000				**£115,000**
2	5	£25,000	£80,000	£55,000	£120,000	£20,000	**£300,000**
3	4	£90,000	£10,000	£15,000	£35,000		**£150,000**
4	3	£200,000	£40,000	£20,000			**£260,000**
5	4	£25,000	£75,000	£40,000	£35,000		**£175,000**
...	...	...	...	...	...	...	...
1000	5	£30,000	£45,000	£120,000	£50,000	£60,000	**£305,000**

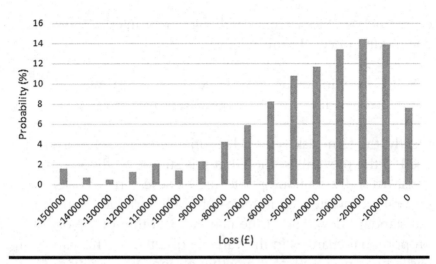

Figure 5.5   Output from Monte-Carlo modelling (1,000 iterations) of annual losses from IT outages

The influence of the lognormal impact distribution is very visible in the long left-hand tail, meaning that there is a not insignificant chance of an enormous loss in a single year. Summary statistics of the distribution are as follows:

■ The expected annual profit/loss = -£480,000;
■ The standard deviation of annual profit/loss = £366,000; and
■ There is a 5% chance of annual losses of greater than £1,150,000.

Distributions Based on Continuous Variation

In contrast to operational risks, which are based on events, many financial risks* concern the continuous evolution of

---

* Specifically, I am considering *passive* financial risks (i.e. risks that non-financial organisations are exposed to in the course of carrying out business), as opposed to value-adding financial risks that financial services firms take on voluntarily.

economic variables such as exchange rates, interest rates and commodity prices. In this context:

- It is meaningless to talk about individual events; and
- Outcomes may be either positive or negative.

Clearly, the term risk is used here in a different sense to that used in the previous section, but it is still perfectly possible to construct a distribution of outcomes. These sorts of risks are generally characterised in terms of "daily volatility", which is the standard deviation of the natural logarithm of the daily proportional changes in the variable of interest. This can then easily be converted into a monthly or annual volatility as required. I will illustrate the construction of a profit and loss distribution with an example using exposure to exchange rate risk below.

Let us suppose that a UK organisation is expecting a payment in US dollars in six months' time; the dollar amount is fixed but, based on today's exchange rate, it would be worth £5 million. The uncertainty in the sterling value of this dollar amount when it is paid in six months represents a risk to the organisation. At the time of writing, the daily volatility of the GBP/USD exchange rate over the last 12 months was approximately 0.7%, and the daily data are a reasonable fit to a normal distribution. This daily volatility translates into a volatility over six months of approximately 8%,* from which one can construct a distribution of potential GBP/USD exchange rates (relative to today's rate) after 6 months. Following the Monte-Carlo approach outlined above one can then draw (1000) random values from this distribution, calculate the value of the fixed dollar amount at each exchange rate and subtract the current sterling value of £5 million to reach a "profit" or "loss" figure. The output from this process is shown in Figure 5.6.

---

* 0.7% multiplied by the square root of 126 (6 months x 21 trading days/month).

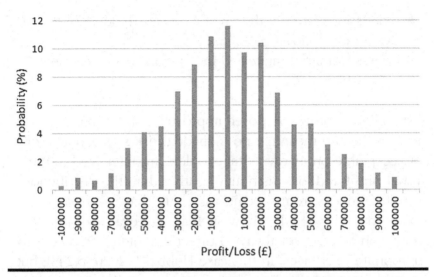

Figure 5.6 Output from Monte-Carlo model (1,000 iterations) of profit and loss from a foreign exchange risk

Once again, there is some roughness in the distribution, which could be removed by running more iterations. Clearly, the shape is very different to the previous example, and this is supported by the following summary statistics:

- The expected profit/loss = -£6,400;
- The standard deviation of profit/loss = £397,000; and
- There is a 5% chance of a loss of greater than £627,000.

So, whilst the standard deviation is very similar to that of the profit and loss distribution from the operational risk example in the previous section, this financial risk makes essentially no difference to expected outcomes, and the likelihood of extreme losses is somewhat less.

Aggregating Profit and Loss Distributions

As stated in Chapter 3, I do not advocate ranking or prioritising individual risks as part of the risk analysis step because:

- One is interested in the impact on stakeholders of the overall portfolio of risks; and
- One is primarily interested in solutions (risk treatments) rather than problems.

In the context of my proposed approach, risk evaluation therefore has no meaning: no individual risk is acceptable or not acceptable on its own. Stakeholders are interested in the overall profit and loss distribution rather than the distributions of profit and loss from specific risks, but I have so far rather glossed over the detail of how such an aggregated distribution is constructed. As always, I direct the interested reader to appropriate references, in this case Hubbard (2020, p.243); but I should like to highlight some important principles.

Before one can combine distributions, they have to be expressed in common units. The impact of IT incidents is very commonly expressed in terms of duration of the outage, whilst the impact of data breaches is often expressed in terms of the number of people affected. As illustrated in the example above, the most common approach is to translate all distributions into monetary units at an early stage. Distasteful as it is to attempt to put a cost on human life or incapacity, this is commonly done in order to allocate resources in many areas of public spending (such as healthcare, transport and the environment), and there is an extensive literature on how to do this. However, in the public and not-for-profit sectors, it may make more sense to measure outcomes and extreme events in non-financial terms,* so the appropriate common unit may be some measure of activity, such as the number of people to whom a service is delivered.

---

* In the risk-taking sidebar in Chapter 1, I gave two real examples of risk management decisions in not-for-profit environments where neither desired outcome was monetary, and in one case the potential losses were measured in injuries and deaths.

When one combines distributions of profits and losses, the expected outcomes simply sum numerically. However, other aspects of the distribution, such as the spread (standard deviation) and likelihood of extreme losses, combine in a much more complex way, depending on to what extent the risks correlate. At one extreme, two risks may be very highly correlated if the underlying causes are similar, e.g. many IT systems will be impacted by any disruption to power supplies, network connectivity or IT infrastructure, so that combining the loss distributions for individual IT systems will greatly increase the spread and the likelihood of extreme losses. At the other extreme, a foreign exchange risk for a UK firm arising from taking payment in US dollars is perfectly negatively correlated with a foreign exchange risk from buying raw materials in US dollars, so combining these two distributions will actually reduce both the overall spread and likelihood of extreme losses. In between these two extremes, many losses will essentially be uncorrelated, and aggregating them will increase the spread and the likelihood of extreme losses more gradually. I illustrate this by combining the profit and loss distribution examples for an operational risk and a financial risk discussed above (Figure 5.7).

Summary statistics for the distribution are as follows:

- The expected annual profit/loss = -£486,000 (simply the sum of the expected losses from the two separate profit and loss distributions);
- The standard deviation of annual profit/loss = £545,000 (much less than the sum of the standard deviations for the two separate loss distributions*); and
- There is a 5% chance of annual losses of greater than £1,378,000.

---

* To be more precise, for uncorrelated distributions such as these, the variances (squares of the standard deviations) are summed.

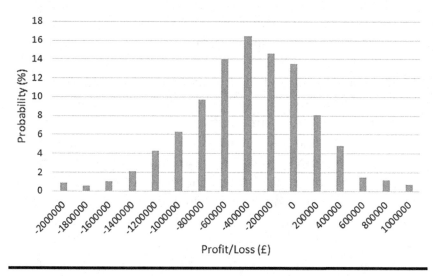

Figure 5.7 Combined profit and loss distribution from operational and financial risks

The focus, in this discussion, is not on value-adding risks but, at least for commercial organisations, I need to include at least one value-adding risk in the overall profit and loss model. Let us consider the example of a small firm, operating in a mature, stable market, where there is only a slight variation in profit from year to year due to ups and downs in demand for different products, selling prices and input costs.[*] Historical data show that the profit (aside from any impact of the operational and financial risks modelled above) is a good fit to a normal distribution with a mean of £800,000 and standard deviation of £100,000. Combining all three profit and loss distributions (once again, assuming no correlation) gives the aggregated distribution shown in Figure 5.8.

Summary statistics for the distribution are as follows:

■ The expected annual profit/loss = £317,000;

---

[*] Presumably the owners of the firm *believe* that they have some competitive advantage in bearing these risks by virtue of their knowledge of the industry.

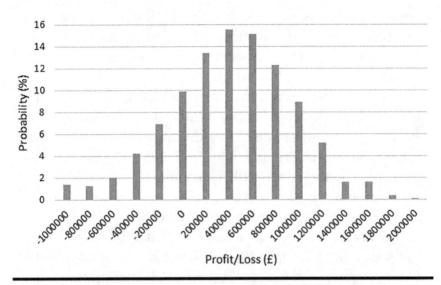

Figure 5.8 Overall profit and loss distribution for the organisation (combining operational, financial and value-adding risks)

- The standard deviation of annual profit/loss = £555,000; and
- There is a 5% chance of annual losses of greater than £585,000.

REPUTATIONAL RISKS SIDEBAR

I broke down the preceding explanation of modelling risks into two sections:

- Modelling risks that manifest themselves as discrete events; and
- Modelling risks that manifest themselves as continuous variation.

In structuring the discussion this way, there was an implied division between "operational" and "financial" risks, but what about the issue of "reputational" risks?

Reputational risks have become very topical in recent years, but discussion of them often lacks clarity, particularly in the definition of what constitutes a reputational risk.

Much of the confusion arises from conflating reputational risks and reputational impacts. Many of the operational risks that organisations face will have reputational impacts if they materialise. Any disruption to services will impact on customers and may lead them to revise their view on whether they wish to continue to transact with the organisation; such revisions will undoubtedly be influenced by negative media coverage. Likewise, a data breach or quality issue, even if it has no immediate impact on the stakeholder groups affected, will likely diminish trust. Often, this reputational damage is a very significant component of the overall impact of an incident, but it can be estimated as part of the process described above for modelling discrete events. Fortunately, by their very nature, these impacts are usually in the public domain, so there are a lot of data available to estimate them.

That still leaves the issue of "pure" reputational risks. These largely concern the discovery, by outsiders, of illegal or dubious business practices such as:

- Bribery and corruption;
- Neglect of environmental and sustainability issues;
- Promotion of products or services damaging to people's mental or physical health;
- Poor labour standards in the supply chain;
- Avoidance of tax or other social responsibilities; or
- Aggressive and/or misleading sales and marketing activities.

So, at the corporate level, the risk will generally depend on both:

- The likelihood that these practices are carrying on somewhere within the organisation without the knowledge of senior management; and
- The likelihood that, if such practices are carrying on, somebody external to the organisation will become aware of this?

The product of these two likelihood estimates can then be combined with an estimated distribution of losses in the event of an incident in the same way that I described previously for modelling discrete events.

Recording and Reporting

Recording and reporting key information is an integral part of the risk analysis step in the risk management process. This largely concerns the details of how modelled distributions have been derived. For models based on empirical data, this should include:

- What internal and external data sources have been used (for how many years);
- Which distributions have been fit to each data set;
- How the best-fitting distribution has been selected; and
- Summary statistics of the selected distributions.

It is also important to document where risks have had to be disaggregated during the risk analysis phase. Alternatively, for models based on expert judgement, information recorded should include:

- Which "experts" were involved in the process;
- What estimation training these experts had received; and
- Which distributions were used, and why?

Recording and reporting this information is essential to provide confidence to stakeholders in the process, to ensure continuity of the programme and to enable continuous improvement.

Summary

This chapter has outlined a quantitative approach to risk assessment, based on some simple modifications to the ISO 31000 risk management process. Specifically, I looked in detail at risk identification and risk analysis (risk evaluation is meaningless in the proposed approach).

Various practical issues with risk identification were discussed, and some examples of risk categorisations were introduced.

I explained how profit and loss distributions for different types of risk can be modelled using Monte-Carlo techniques, and then aggregated into an overall profit and loss distribution for the organisation.

The idea of compiling an aggregated profit and loss distribution for the organisation will probably seem rather daunting at first, but don't despair! Even if, at first, the model only includes a few of the most important risks, it will still be a vast improvement on previous qualitative approaches. Indeed, as I will explain in the next chapter, it is possible to perform an initial evaluation of some risk treatments using only the profit and loss distributions for a single risk.

References

Cope E, 2010, Modeling Operational Loss Severity Distributions from Consortium Data, *The Journal of Operational Risk*, 5(4): 35–64.

Cruz M, 2002, *Modelling, Measuring and Hedging Operational Risk*, Chichester: John Wiley & Sons.

Dahen H and Dionne G, 2010, Scaling Models for the Severity and Frequency of External Operational Loss Data, *Journal of Banking and Finance*, 34: 1484–1496.

Elliott D, Swartz E and Herbane B, 2002, *Business Continuity Management: A Crisis Management Approach*, London: Routledge.

Hubbard D, 2020, *The Failure of Risk Management: Why it's Broken and How to Fix It*, 2nd Edition, Hoboken, NJ: Wiley.

LAS, 2017, *Report on the New Year's Day 2017 Computer Aided Dispatch System Outage*, London Ambulance Service. Available at https://www.londonambulance.nhs.uk/wp-content/uploads/2018/04/New-Years-Day-CAD-outage-report-27-June-2017.pdf (downloaded 22/09/21).

Merton R, 2005, You Have More Capital Than You Think, *Harvard Business Review*, November 2005: 84–94.

Okoroh MI, Gombera PP and Alani AM, 2002, Managing Risks in the UK Healthcare Sector, *Risk Management: An International Journal*, 4(3): 43–58.

Taleb N, 2007, *The Black Swan*, London: Allen Lane.

Chapter 6

Risk Treatment

I have emphasised repeatedly up to now that the focus of risk management should be on risk treatments rather than the risks themselves: in this chapter, I finally turn to look at risk treatment in detail. I have also emphasised that risk treatment decisions should be made on the same basis as any other decision within the organisation, that is, on the basis of return on investment. In an idealised world, organisations make economically optimal decisions but, in reality, organisations usually proceed by satisficing, not optimising. In particular, this involves setting a level for what is an acceptable return on investment for projects to proceed: the following discussion of decisions about risk treatments takes this approach throughout.

I illustrate the risk treatment process below with a worked example of a single risk reduction being applied. I will consider the return on investment of this particular risk reduction in the same three stages that I have used up until now: the effect on expected outcomes, reducing the likelihood of extreme losses and reducing variability in outcomes. This

DOI: 10.4324/9781003225157-6

is followed by a short discussion of the issues involved in combining different risk treatments, and the chapter concludes with some guidance on what information needs to be recorded and reported as part of the risk treatment stage of the overall risk management process.

I will illustrate the process of evaluating a risk treatment using the overall profit and loss distribution derived in Chapter 5 (Figure 5.8), combining an operational risk (IT outage), a financial risk (foreign exchange) and a value-adding risk.* I will assume that the precise effect of a particular risk reduction is known in advance, in order to calculate the value of implementing it to different stakeholder groups. Of course, in reality, risk treatments are themselves risky investments with uncertain outcomes: I will return to the question of measuring the outcomes of risk treatments in Chapter 7.

Modelling the Risk Treatment

Let us suppose that a risk reduction has been proposed (e.g. a software upgrade or a new server) that would reduce the average annual number of IT outages from five to four.† The first stage in the evaluation of the risk treatment is to run a new Monte-Carlo simulation (once again 1,000 iterations are used in this illustration) based on the reduced average number of outages. The profit and loss distribution before and after risk reduction is shown in Figure 6.1.

It is immediately clear from the graph that the risk reduction has resulted in a lower probability of very high losses.

---

* An alternative example in the context of a public sector/not-for-profit organisation is contained at Annex C.
† I will return in Chapter 7 to look at how one can establish if this projected gain has in fact been achieved. Other possible risk reductions may aim to reduce the impact of disruptions but have no effect on their incidence (see example at Annex C), or may aim to reduce both the incidence and impact of disruptions.

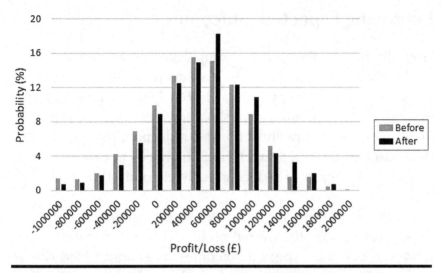

Figure 6.1 Comparison of profit and loss distributions before and after risk treatment

The summary statistics of the distribution give us more information, as follows:

- The expected annual profit/loss is increased from £317,000 to £401,000;
- The standard deviation of annual profit/loss is reduced from £555,000 to £521,000; and
- There is a 5% chance of annual losses of greater than £454,000.

One now needs to look at the value to stakeholders of each of these changes in more detail. Calculating the value of improvements in expected outcomes is relatively straightforward because the savings are completely independent of the ownership structure of the organisation. However, this is not the case for reducing the likelihood of extreme losses or reducing the variability in outcomes, so, in these cases, one has to look separately at the value of the risk reduction to different types of organisations.

Improving Expected Outcomes

From the figures above, it can immediately be seen that implementing the proposed risk reduction yields an increase in expected profit of approximately *£84,000* annually. If this exceeds the organisation's threshold for return on the investment required to implement the risk reduction, then it has been justified straight away. If not, one needs to proceed to consider the impact of reducing the likelihood of extreme losses.

Ultimately, stakeholders are interested in the impact of a risk treatment on the overall profit and loss distribution. However, because expected outcomes are simply added when profit and loss distributions are combined, the impact of risk treatments on expected outcomes can actually be modelled on the individual risks that they are intended to mitigate. This observation is very important, as it allows an organisation to establish a business case for some risk treatments even before risk modelling is complete. Thus, some "quick wins" can be implemented and evaluated immediately which, in turn, generates data on the effectiveness of the overall risk management programme to justify further investment in the programme.

Reducing the Likelihood of Extreme Events

In Chapter 4, focusing specifically on reducing the likelihood of losses large enough to trigger bankruptcy, I calculated that, for the small firm in that example, it is worth paying at least £11,000/year for a 1% reduction in the likelihood of sustaining a loss of greater than £600,000. The proposed risk reduction has reduced the probability of such a loss from 4.7% to 3.3%, so is worth at least £15,000. If the total annual benefits of the proposed risk reduction of approximately *£99,000* are now sufficient to justify the investment required, one can halt the analysis there. If not, it may be worth looking in more detail at the benefits to various other stakeholder groups (e.g. employees, customers, suppliers) of reducing the likelihood of bankruptcy.

Clearly, for a not-for-profit organisation, with no owners, the corresponding value of such a reduction in the likelihood of bankruptcy would be somewhat less, driven primarily by the reduction in the cost of debt. In this context, it is also important to bear in mind the potential value of reducing the likelihood of non-financial extreme events.

Reducing the Variability in Outcomes

To complete the illustration, I look finally at the benefits to stakeholders from reducing the variability in outcomes. As discussed previously, the impact of variability depends entirely on the ownership structure of the organisation. Given the complexity of the arguments involved, a business case for risk management reliant on quantifying the benefits of reducing variability in outcomes is much more open to challenge, so is best avoided if at all possible. I will start by looking at the example of an entrepreneurial firm, with one or more owners heavily invested in it, and then discuss how one can approach the calculation for other types of organisations.

Entrepreneurial Firms

Directly applying the risk criterion derived in Chapter 4 from utility theory, in the context of a small firm, reducing the standard deviation from £555,000 to £521,000 could be worth another £90,000 to the owners of the business. However, given the various reservations about this very theoretical approach, I would advocate an alternative **bootstrapping** technique, based on the profit and loss model that was developed in

Chapter 5 (Figure 5.8). This has the important advantage that the value of the risk reduction is inferred from the actual decisions being taken by the firms' managers (presumably incorporating the wishes of other stakeholder groups) in the current economic climate.

The standard deviation of the profit/loss distribution (without risk reduction) is approximately £555,000, and the expected annual profit is approximately £317,000.* Logically, this risk/return ratio should capture the preferences of stakeholders, so one should aim to maintain this ratio. Based on this ratio, an extra £570 of expected profit is required for every additional £1,000 of variability in profit. Or, put another way, a £1,000 reduction in variability is worth about £570. Thus, a reduction in the standard deviation of £34,000 is worth about £19,000, a far lower figure than the one obtained above from applying utility theory directly. Thus, for this entrepreneurial firm, the total value of the proposed risk reduction is approximately **£118,000** a year.

Corporations

As discussed in some detail in Chapter 1, well-diversified investors are primarily interested in the covariance of returns with the market as a whole, not the actual variation of returns. Generally speaking, operational risks will be largely uncorrelated with market returns, whilst financial risks and value-adding risks may be correlated with them. When calculating the value of reducing variability in outcomes, it is therefore

---

* Technically, one should calculate the return over the risk-free rate. If, as discussed above, the profit of £317 000 is derived from an asset base including £600 000 of shareholders' equity, then the return on equity (ROE) is about 53%, a not unreasonable return to investors in the current environment. With interest rates currently at historic lows of around 1%, this corresponds to a return over a risk-free investment of approximately 52%, so, in this case, the adjustment is trivial.

incorrect to aggregate all types of risk in the manner illustrated above: one has to clearly separate those risks that are correlated with the market and those that are not. It would absolutely not be in the interests of these investors if a firm were to take on significant additional value-adding risk (which might be highly correlated with the market) in response to a decrease in operational risk (the impact of which they can greatly reduce simply by diversification).*

For the purposes of this illustration, I will make the simplifying assumption that operational, financial and value-adding risks are all uncorrelated with the market. The empirical studies discussed in Chapter 4 found that stock market investors required roughly a 1% increase in annual returns for each 4% increase in the variability of returns not correlated with the market. So, a reduction in standard deviation of £34,000 would only be worth approximately £9,000 to well-diversified investors. Although it is important to reiterate that this figure is a long-term average, and will almost certainly vary over time as economic conditions change. Thus, for a firm owned by well-diversified investors, the total value of the proposed risk reduction is approximately **£107,000** a year.

Whilst theoretically possible, it is not straightforward to apply the bootstrapping approach outlined in the previous section to large companies, where ownership is by well-diversified shareholders.

Public Sector and Not-for-Profit Organisations

In Chapter 1, I discussed a number of reasons why minimising variation in outcomes was desirable in all sectors. As well as minimising adjustment costs, I argued that one of the reasons to seek to minimise variation was to ensure that internal funds are always available to respond effectively to opportunities

---

* I return to this point in the context of the impact of Covid-19 in Annex B.

and demands, as and when they arise. Even though delivering a surplus is not an end in itself, this would suggest that reducing the variability in the surplus is of value, particularly to the management team, in order to ensure a reliable stream of internal funds to finance planned future activity. One can use exactly the same bootstrapping approach as outlined above for the entrepreneurial firm, simply substituting "surplus" for "profit", to quantify the value of reducing variability. One simply infers from the model what increase in surplus the organisation's stakeholders require in return for a given increase in variability in that surplus. As above, this is equivalent to inferring how much stakeholders are willing to pay for a given reduction in variability. Whilst I will not attempt to quantify a risk/return ratio for a non-profit organisation here, the risk reduction will presumably be worth even less than the £9,000 value to well-diversified investors calculated above.

Some Parting Observations

This concludes this illustrative example of quantifying the benefits of a risk treatment, but, recalling the discussion in Chapter 2, it is important to remember that there may be additional benefits that are less straightforward to estimate. Regrettably, the example has become somewhat bogged down in the minutiae of calculating the value of reducing the variability of outcomes under different ownership structures. Hopefully, if nothing else, this has demonstrated that recourse to arguments based on reducing the variability of outcomes is complex and open to challenges, so it really is a last resort. It also suggests that, aside from the special case of an entrepreneurial firm, the value derived from reducing the variability in outcomes is likely to be a relatively small component of the overall value to stakeholders of a risk treatment.

Combining Risk Treatments

The effect of any particular risk treatment on the overall loss distribution also depends on what other risk treatments are being applied as risk treatments may interact with each other. By way of an illustration, improved technical security measures and increased staff awareness will both affect the frequency and loss distributions for cyber-attacks, and thus the overall loss distribution. However, the effects are not necessarily additive: that is, the impact of improving technical security measures *and* increasing staff awareness may well be less than the sum of the impacts of applying each risk treatment separately. I have already highlighted how generic contingency planning (such as business continuity management or crisis management) can yield a very good return on investment; however, the value of such programmes will depend significantly on the extent to which individual risks (e.g. fire, flood, supply chain disruption) are also being mitigated. Bear in mind also that each risk treatment changes the overall profit and loss distribution, so the estimated value will depend on what other risk treatments are applied. Clearly though, if one had to evaluate each possible combination of risk treatments, the task would be immense. Some pragmatism is therefore required in identifying where there may be significant interactions between risk treatments, and evaluating different combinations of these, whilst many other treatments can, for practical purposes, be evaluated in isolation.

Recording and Reporting

As with each of the previous stages in the risk management process, recording and reporting certain key information is an integral part of risk treatment. This should, as a minimum, include details of:

■ Which individual risk treatments and what combinations of these risk treatments have been considered,
■ Why specific combinations were chosen for implementation, and
■ What the expected outcomes of these treatments are.

Summary

This chapter concludes the description of a proposed, quantitative approach to risk management by looking at how risk treatments can be evaluated. The output from this process is an estimate of the return on investment for various combinations of risk treatments. If this return on investment is above an acceptable level, then the risk treatment(s) should be implemented.

An example of one specific risk reduction was evaluated based on its impact on expected outcomes, probability of extreme losses and variability of outcomes. It is important to note that the value of improving expected outcomes can be calculated on individual profit and loss distributions, even before these are aggregated. The benefits of reducing variability in outcomes are entirely dependent on the nature of ownership, and are the most difficult to quantify.

It is important to be mindful of the potential for risk treatments to interact but, in practice, it should not be necessary to evaluate every possible combination of risk treatments.

Chapter 7

Measuring the Effectiveness of Risk Management

One of my main criticisms of prevailing risk management practices is the lack of a solid evidence basis for which approaches and specific interventions work. Indeed, there seems to be an astonishing lack of curiosity about what actually works: in over 15 years of delivering different risk management projects for clients, I cannot think of an example of a client who had a clear idea of how they would measure the return on investment for a project. How should this problem be addressed?

I should like to look at the question of measuring the effectiveness of risk management from various different perspectives. I shall begin by looking at directly measuring the effectiveness of individual risk treatments. I shall then review the evidence for whether prior risk management activity demonstrates measurable benefits when organisations actually have to deal with major incidents. Following the discussion in Chapter 3 of integrated risk management, in this chapter I

DOI: 10.4324/9781003225157-7

also look at the idea of measuring progress towards achieving this paradigm as another way of assessing the effectiveness of risk management. Finally, I look at measuring the overall impact of risk management programmes on the value of firms. Ultimately, I suggest that there are limitations and caveats with all of these measurement approaches and that, in practice, one often has to triangulate from multiple techniques to draw any useful conclusions.

Whilst acknowledging the significant difficulties involved, it cannot be over-emphasised that measurement is an ongoing, integral part of any risk management programme, not some sort of optional add-on. As discussed in Chapter 4, the resources committed to risk management need to be justified; generally, this will involve measuring the costs and benefits of the programme as it is rolled out incrementally. However, even when a risk management programme is well-established, it is important to continually monitor that it is still delivering value for money.

Measuring the Effectiveness of Individual Risk Treatments

In the numerical example in Chapter 6, a risk treatment was modelled that was claimed to reduce the annual incidence of outages of a particular IT system from five to four. Having implemented such a risk reduction, one would presumably wish to evaluate if the desired effect had been achieved. Sadly, measuring the effectiveness of an individual risk reduction such as this is not entirely straightforward. As mentioned in Chapter 6, individual risk treatments may yield very uncertain returns, although, in aggregate, these uncertainties tend to balance each other out.

Even if the "true" long-term average frequency had been reduced to four, there is still a 37% chance of five or more

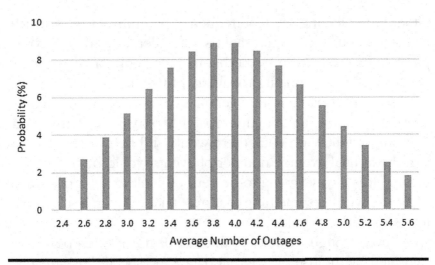

Figure 7.1 Distribution of average frequency of outages over a five-year period following risk treatment

outages in any given year: one can easily imagine the embarrassment for all concerned if, after making a considerable investment to reduce the number of outages, the number of disruptions actually increases in the following year. The distribution of the average frequency of outages over five years, if the true frequency was indeed reduced to four by the risk treatment, is shown in Figure 7.1. Whilst there is a good chance of demonstrating an improvement over the historical average of five outages per year, potentially a very large one, there is still a 16% chance that this will not happen.

Unfortunately, the difficulty of demonstrating the effectiveness of individual risk treatments may present a significant barrier to investing in risk management.* Not only does this measurement challenge likely reduce the overall appetite for risk management, but it also constitutes a perverse incentive to focus on managing routine risks, where it will be relatively easy to demonstrate an improvement in a realistic time frame,

---

* Recall the perspectives from the *Behavioral Theory of the Firm* in the discussion in Chapter 2 about reasons not to adopt risk management.

rather than tackling the low-frequency/high-impact risks which can actually destroy organisations. Consider, by way of a comparison, the case of an event that happens only once every two years (i.e. an annual probability of 0.5). If one implemented a risk treatment that genuinely reduced this to once every 3 years (i.e. an annual probability of 0.333) and gathered 20 years of follow-up data, there would still be a 14% chance that the annual average number of events would be 0.5 or greater. It is always going to be very difficult to get a commitment to invest in something that may take 20 years (or more) to demonstrate its value.

As ever though, scarcity of internal data can often be mitigated by the use of external data. One specific risk treatment that has been extensively researched in the academic literature is the use of derivatives to transfer risk. For example, Allayannis and Weston (2001) found that US firms that were exposed to foreign exchange risk were valued 5% higher (by the market) if they used derivatives. Similarly, Perez-Gonzalez and Yun (2013) found that US utilities firms that used weather derivatives were valued 6% higher. So even if, in the short term, your own derivatives programme is not delivering the returns that you had expected, you can still have confidence that it will prove of value in the longer term.

Estimating the Mitigating Effect on Major Disruptions

Clearly, it is not going to be possible to demonstrate that measures taken to reduce the likelihood or impact of a once-in-a-lifetime event have made a positive return on investment in any meaningful timescale using the modelling approach outlined above. Moreover, I suggested in Chapter 3 that generic contingency planning to mitigate the effects of a wide range of different events often offers better return on investment than specific actions to try to reduce the likelihood (and/or impact) of specific events. In this section, I therefore review the evidence for any mitigating effect of more general risk treatments, and indeed entire risk management programmes, when organisations have actually had to deal with major disruptions.

Knight and Pretty (1996, 2005) have done much interesting work in this field. However, it is important to note that these studies have never been published in academic journals, and that the studies have generally been sponsored by organisations that have a commercial interest in the findings. Their earliest studies looked at a number of high-profile corporate crises and tracked the affected companies' share prices for a year after the event. All share prices fell immediately after the event, but the study identified that some then recovered strongly, leading to a considerable gap (approximately 25% of market value) between the fortunes of "recoverer" and "non-recoverer" firms a year after a crisis. This *suggested* that some firms were much better prepared to deal with a crisis than others; the authors highlighted in particular the importance of effective communications, but no actual hypotheses were tested in these early studies. (see Whatever Became of Knight and Pretty's "Recoverers" and "Non-Recoverers" side-bar) However, in Knight and Pretty (2005), the authors specifically tested the hypothesis that airlines retaining a specialist services provider to assist in managing mass casualty incidents protected shareholder value. In their study of the impact of 22 mass-fatality aviation disasters on the airlines involved, they found that the share price of half of the sample that retained such a specialist provider outperformed those that didn't by 40%. It is important to stress though that no attempt was made in the analysis to compensate for other differences between the two groups. It is therefore quite possible that the observed gulf in performance between the two groups of airlines arose because of some unobserved underlying difference (for example, it could be that the high-performing airlines were fundamentally better managed) and not the retaining of a specialist provider.

Whatever Became of Knight and Pretty's "Recoverers" and "Non-Recoverers"?

As mentioned above, Knight and Pretty's early studies did not actually test any specific hypotheses: they merely observed the performance of firms following a crisis and noted that some companies performed much better than others. Interestingly, in Knight and Pretty (1996), Johnson & Johnson appears twice: once as a recoverer and once as a non-recoverer. The fact that Johnson & Johnson appears as a non-recoverer following the Tylenol poisoning in 1982 but as a recoverer following another Tylenol poisoning four years later could be because the company learnt valuable lessons from the first incident and improved its crisis management capability. But it could also be that outcomes are largely driven by the specific details of the crisis, and other external factors (e.g. what other news stories are prominent at the time), and have little to do with firms' inherent crisis management capabilities.

I was developing a crisis management presentation with a partner organisation some years ago and I was explaining to my colleagues about the 1996 study. As I started listing some of the recoverers, one of my colleagues looked troubled and pointed out that a number of these companies no longer existed! Needless to say, we glossed over this detail in the presentation, but it did reignite the question of whether the distinction between recoverers and non-recoverers observed in the 1996 study actually told us anything of value about the companies themselves.

It would be fascinating to conduct a longer-term study of how the different groups of firms performed, to establish if the recoverers truly possessed some persistent advantage, but this is simply not possible as so many of the companies no longer exist in their original form. What I can say is that, of the original seven recoverers in the 1996 study (not counting J&J), only two (Heineken and Sandoz) exist in the same form as of February 2021. Of the remaining five firms:

■ Pan Am filed for bankruptcy in 1991;
■ Upjohn merged with Pharmacia AB in 1995;
■ Commercial Union merged with General Accident in 1998;
■ Philips Petroleum merged with Conoco in 2002; and
■ P&O was bought by DP World in 2006.

Turning to the six non-recoverers (once again, not counting J&J), three of them still exist in the same form: Eli Lilly, Occidental and Shell. Of the remaining three:

■ Perrier was bought by Nestle in 1992;
■ Exxon merged with Mobil in 1999; and
■ Union Carbide was bought by Dow Chemicals in 2001.

It would take a great deal of additional work to understand why these firms were bought or merged, and establish what this implied about their long-term performance. But, just on the basis of this very superficial analysis, it would appear that being identified as a recoverer in the 1996 study does not confer any long-term survival advantage.

Ellul and Yerramilli (2013) explored the mitigating effect of formal risk management systems in their study of US banks during the credit crunch of 2007-2008. They constructed a measure of the maturity of each firm's risk management, prior to 2007, based on factors such as the existence of a Chief Risk Officer position, the remuneration of the Chief Risk Officer, the experience of the risk committee and the activity of the risk committee. They then observed various performance measures over the evolution of the credit crunch. As well as experiencing fewer non-performing loans, banks with stronger risk management frameworks (prior to the onset of the crisis) demonstrated higher average returns to shareholders and less extreme daily losses to shareholders during the crisis.

I have also undertaken some research in this area myself, looking at the impact of the Covid-19 pandemic on the share prices of UK FTSE 100 companies from February 2020 to February 2021 (full details of this study are contained in Annex B). The focus of the research was to test the hypothesis that firms that have adopted good practice in business continuity management, as proxied by employing a member of the Business Continuity Institute (BCI), would perform better during the pandemic. Nineteen firms were identified that definitely employed one or more members of the BCI, although this is very likely to be something of an underestimate. Initially there was no significant effect of employing a BCI member, in the early months of the pandemic the main drivers of changes in share price were:

- The extent to which the firm's share price normally co-varied with the market as a whole; and
- The industry sector in which they operated.

Unsurprisingly, firms in the travel and leisure industry were particularly badly hit, whilst pharmaceutical firms performed relatively strongly. However, after about six months, a statistically significant effect of employing BCI members emerged: surprisingly though the effect was *negative, reaching -14.9%* of firm value by February 2021.

Whilst analysing crises is superficially appealing, and useful in other ways, it is clearly a very inexact way of measuring the return on investment of an individual risk treatment or programme of risk treatments. Whilst the findings of both Knight and Pretty (2005) and Ellul and Yerramilli (2013) are encouraging in suggesting that risk management is of value when an organisation experiences a crisis, it is important to stress that:

■ There was no attempt to establish a causal relationship; and
■ There was no attempt to quantify the likelihood of such a crisis occurring.

As regards Knight and Pretty (2005), one would also need to explore whether alternative risk treatments, such as measures to reduce the likelihood of a mass-fatality incident, offered better value for money. Conversely, whilst the results of the Covid-19 study are both surprising and disappointing (to say the least), the observed negative impact of employing a member of the BCI does not necessarily mean that a well-designed business continuity management programme will not deliver good value for money in the long term (this point is discussed in detail in Annex B).

Evaluating the Success of Implementation

Stepping back from direct measures of the financial impact of risk management, another perspective on measuring the "effectiveness" of a programme is to investigate if the agreed policies and procedures are being applied throughout the organisation in order to achieve the aims of integrated risk management (as discussed in Chapter 3). Whilst I have repeatedly criticised the compliance approach of some practitioners throughout this book, I have also emphasised that an appropriate amount of monitoring, reviewing, recording and reporting is actually very important. In particular, it is necessary to monitor if:

- Managers at all levels are taking ownership of risks within their area of responsibility;
- A consistent risk appetite is being applied (to both risk management and risk-taking decisions) throughout the organisation;
- Data are being gathered and models are being updated and validated; and
- The effectiveness of risk treatments is being measured.

Awareness of all of these factors will enable continuous improvements to be made in order to optimise effectiveness. It is also very important to ensure that training is taking place and that contingency plans are being regularly tested and exercised. However, my central critique of the compliance approach remains: even achieving perfect alignment with an idealised model of integrated risk management does not prove that value has actually been created (for any stakeholder groups). The cost of implementing a "perfect" programme may simply outweigh the benefits achieved.

Quantifying the Overall Impact of Risk Management Programmes

Ultimately, one aims to quantify the overall impact on the organisation of investing in risk management (whether or not any disruptions occur). In theory, one could aggregate the effects of each individual risk treatment and subtract any central costs of the risk management programme (e.g. staff costs). However, this fails to capture any broader positive effect (e.g. an improvement in the organisation's reputation or the ability to win more business) from the overall risk management programme. Studying crises is also an imperfect measure of the overall impact of a risk management programme, as:

- Risk management activities should also create benefit by reducing the likelihood of disruptions; and
- Even if some form of risk management demonstrates a benefit in a crisis, one needs to also factor in the likelihood of an organisation experiencing such a crisis (which, by definition, is very difficult to quantify) to estimate the overall long-term benefit.

I have also discussed measuring how well a risk management programme has been implemented, and concluded that this is very important in terms of optimising effectiveness, but it cannot actually determine if the programme is value-creating or value-destroying. It is not possible to measure the overall effect of a risk management programme on an individual organisation's performance, as one cannot separate out the effect of this from all the other factors impacting on performance. The best that one can do is to look at a sample of firms, some of which have adopted the approach to risk management of interest, and compare performance between adopters and non-adopters. Thus, measuring the impact of risk management programmes is generally the preserve of academics rather than practitioners.

Estimating the overall impact of risk management programmes has traditionally been approached, in the context of corporations, by measuring the effect on shareholder value: clearly this is not possible to do with smaller firms or with public sector and not-for-profit organisations. As well as the difficulty, discussed in Chapter 2, of determining what is meant by organisations "adopting" risk management, when trying to measure the impact of risk management programmes there is a significant additional challenge, the difficulty of separating out cause and effect. As discussed in the previous section on the impact of crises, one could observe that adoption of risk management is associated with higher performance because risk management improves performance, or because well-managed, high-performing firms are more likely to adopt innovations such as risk management. Simply observing an association cannot determine which one it is, or indeed whether it is some combination of both.

Many different studies have looked specifically at the impact of adoption of enterprise risk management (ERM) on firm value. Adoption of ERM has generally been measured in the same way as discussed in Chapter 2, based on publicly available information about the firm's risk management activities or self-reported data. A number of these studies have found statistically significant, positive effects on firm value of up to 25% (Farrell and Gallagher (2015)) from implementing ERM. However, as well as the previous caveat about separating cause and effect,[*] it is important to bear in mind the bias towards publishing studies with statistically significant results in academic journals: there may be even greater numbers of studies that found no effect on firm value but that never got published. So, the published figures may very well be an overestimate.

Frankly, at the top end of this range, these figures just seem too good to be true. Given that, in any sample of firms, some will be implementing risk management much better than others,[†] if the average over all adopters is a 25% increase in value, it implies that some will be achieving even greater increases than this. It just seems implausible that firms would be realising gains approaching 50% of firm value simply from adopting ERM. Furthermore, Sprcic et al. (2016) find that

---

[*] A discussion of the various empirical methods that different studies have adopted to try to address this issue is beyond the scope of this book.

[†] See the discussion about variability in the quality of implementation of risk management in Chapter 3.

whilst firms experience a temporary increase in value when they adopt ERM, this peaks after a couple of years and begins to fall away again. Nevertheless, it is very encouraging to see a growing body of evidence that suggests that adopting risk management does have a positive impact on firm value.

Taking a Pragmatic Approach to Measurement

Monitoring and reviewing is a critical step in the risk management process but, as I have discussed in detail in this chapter, there are significant challenges in measuring the effectiveness of risk management. These challenges are most pronounced in the early stages of implementation when data are scarce. It is therefore very important at the outset, in developing the risk management framework (see Chapter 3), to be clear on how effectiveness will be measured. This will involve:

- Being clear on what data are needed to inform risk management decisions;
- Agreeing on what internal data need to be collected and by whom;
- Identifying where relevant external data can be sourced and how they can be combined with internal data;
- Agreeing on appropriate confidence intervals for drawing conclusions – conventional academic thresholds of 95% (or greater) confidence are unlikely to be achievable in any realistic timescale.

Multiple measurement methods will usually be required, in different combinations over the lifecycle of the risk management programme. Initially, in developing the business case for risk management, there will be a heavy reliance on external data, using results from commercial surveys and/or academic research to guide decision-making. In the early years of the programme, the emphasis will probably be on measuring the success of implementing and embedding risk management. However, data on the effectiveness of individual risk treatments, possibly augmented by pooling data with peers, will be building up all the time. Being able to demonstrate that even a few specific risk treatments have had the desired effect will significantly boost confidence in the programme. Along the way there may, unfortunately, be occasions when business continuity plans, crisis management plans or similar have to be invoked. Even though it will never be possible to say with absolute certainty how the result was different to what it would have been without the plan, a thorough post-incident review will yield a good sense of the extent to which impacts were mitigated, as well as identifying further opportunities for improvement. Even within the context of corporations, it is not possible to measure the effect on value of an individual firm implementing risk management, as overall performance is determined by a whole array of factors. However, other organisation-wide measures, such as customer satisfaction, may provide further evidence of the value of risk management.

Summary

The nature of random sampling presents real challenges to measuring the effectiveness of individual risk treatments, particularly those relating to low-frequency/high-impact events. As well as being a general disincentive to invest in risk management, this constitutes a perverse incentive to focus on treating routine risks rather than the risks that could really damage the organisation. In some cases, this problem can be mitigated through the use of external data from academic studies.

Studies of firms in crisis offer an alternative perspective on the effectiveness of risk management. There is strong support for the effectiveness of very specific contingency planning, but mixed results for more general risk management programmes.

Measuring how consistently risk management policies and processes are being applied is very important in terms of optimising effectiveness but cannot, on its own, demonstrate if the programme is creating value.

A number of studies have found very impressive effects from the implementation of risk management, specifically ERM, on firm value. However, the combination of difficulties in separating out cause and effect, and a publication bias towards statistically significant results, suggests that the higher figures, up to 25% increase in firm value, may be an overestimate of the true effect size.

Given the difficulties involved in measuring the effectiveness of risk management, I advocate a pragmatic approach, using multiple methods and making use of external data wherever possible.

References

Allayannis G and Weston J, 2001, The Use of Foreign Currency Derivatives and Firm Market Value, *The Review of Financial Studies*, 14(1): 243–276.

Ellul A and Yerramilli V, 2013, Stronger Risk Controls, Lower Risk: Evidence from U.S. Bank Holding Companies, *Journal of Finance*, 68(5): 1757–1803.

Farrell M and Gallagher R, 2015, The Valuation Implications of Enterprise Risk Management Maturity, *Journal of Risk and Insurance*, 82(3): 625–657.

Knight R and Pretty D, 1996, *The Impact of Catastrophes on Shareholder Value*, Templeton College, University of Oxford. Available at http://www.michaelsamonas.gr/images/Mixalhs/resources/Impact_of_Catastophes_on_Shareholder_Value.pdf (downloaded 22/06/2021).

Knight R and Pretty D, 2005, *Protecting Value in the Face of Mass Fatality Events*, Oxford Metrica. Available at http://oxfordmetrica.com/public/CMS/Files/601/04RepComKen.pdf (downloaded 22/06/2021).

Perez-Gonzalez F and Yun H, 2013, Risk Management and Firm Value: Evidence from Weather Derivatives, *Journal of Finance*, 68(5): 2143–2176.

Sprcic D, Zagar M, Sevic Z and Marc M, 2016, Does Enterprise Risk Management Influence Market Value - A Long-Term Perspective, *Risk Management: An International Journal*, 18(2–3): 65–88.

Chapter 8

Underlying Themes and Summary

Following the discussion of some fundamental ideas about risk in Chapters 1 and 2, Chapter 3 introduced the concepts of risk management systems and integrated risk management. Chapters 4-6 then proceeded to outline a straightforward, quantitative process for risk management. Successful implementation is entirely dependent on having effective monitoring in place, and Chapter 7 explored this critical question of how one measures if individual risk treatments, and indeed the overall risk management programme, are delivering value. In this final chapter, I explore some themes and practical issues that span multiple stages of the risk management process and have thus not been covered in detail in previous chapters. These themes include the link between strategy and risk, where risk management fits within the organisation, crises and black-swans and the applicability of quantitative techniques in the public and not-for-profit sectors. These discussions are followed by a critical review of how the approach outlined in this book could have informed preparations for and responses to Covid-19, and the chapter concludes with a summary of the

DOI: 10.4324/9781003225157-8

key ideas that I have tried to put across in this book. I begin though, by tackling head-on some of the common arguments against quantitative risk management.

Is a Quantitative Approach Really Practical?

Whilst I say above that my proposed quantitative approach is straightforward, clearly it will take some time to implement fully. Risk management sometimes appears to be embarked upon with an air of dread and panic: as if there are numerous imminent existential threats to the organisation which must be dealt with urgently. It should be borne in mind though that, in most cases, the organisation has been operating successfully for a period of time. This suggests that if any such existential threats exist, they are probably already being managed to some extent, albeit informally. I would therefore argue that it is worth taking the time to implement risk management properly, in a quantitative manner, rather than rushing to implement a beguilingly simple qualitative approach. However, I am very aware that others will argue that a quantitative approach is simply not practical.

Those opposed to the approach outlined in this book may well argue that it is impossible to identify all the risks to which an organisation is exposed, and that data will be too scarce on many of these risks to apply quantitative methods. The first argument is simply a statement of the blindingly obvious, and applies equally to any approach to risk management. (I will discuss the specific issue of rare and extreme events below.) Simply stating that you are following some form of widely accepted good practice, with a lot of documentation, does not change the fact that your knowledge of the risks that the organisation faces is necessarily incomplete. The second argument generally derives from a fundamental misunderstanding of quantitative techniques. Specifically, there are widespread misconceptions about the concept of statistical significance, leading to an erroneous belief that large quantities of data are required in order to draw any useful conclusions. Crucially, a quantitative approach actively highlights where information is lacking and what data need to be gathered, whereas qualitative approaches merely gloss over this uncomfortable truth. Ultimately, as I have highlighted many times throughout the text, much of risk management boils down to a commitment to gathering and analysing data on an ongoing basis.

The experience of pioneers in this field, such as Douglas Hubbard (see Hubbard (2020)), demonstrates categorically that a quantitative approach to risk management is achievable in a wide range of organisations. My own experience is that all sorts of organisations, from NHS Trusts to small manufacturing companies, already have a great deal of useful risk data, far more than they sometimes realise. Hopefully, this book will help to give people the confidence to apply those data in quantitative risk models. Ultimately, the best evidence of the practicality of the approach outlined in this book will be your own experience. Throughout this book, I have actively embraced the idea of an incremental approach to becoming more quantitative about risk management. Beginning with data that already exist in the organisation, one can start by quantitatively analysing some of the most visible risks first. As discussed in Chapter 6, a simple evaluation of a risk treatment based solely on the changes to expected outcomes can be conducted on individual risks, even before an aggregated profit and loss distribution has been constructed. As people gain confidence that the quantitative approach is practical and is delivering value, one can gradually tackle the risks for which less data are currently available and begin to conduct the evaluation of risk treatments in a more rigorous manner.

How Does Strategy Link to Risk?

One of the main themes throughout this book has been that risk management decisions should be viewed as normal business decisions, taken in the context of the organisation's overall strategy. Clearly, the organisation's strategy will influence all aspects of the risk management process from discussions on risk criteria to decisions as to how to measure the effectiveness of a major risk management programme. But, equally, the understanding of the risks that an organisation faces, and how they can be managed (and at what cost), will influence what strategy is adopted, so there is a broader question of how risk and strategy interact. Unfortunately, the practitioner literature is mysteriously silent on this point, beyond general statements such as "The risk management process should be aligned with the organization's culture, processes, structure and strategy" (ISO (2009, para 5.3.3)). However, the academic literature offers a number of different (stakeholder) views on the relationship between strategy and risk which will be discussed very briefly below.

Within the strategy literature, taking the perspective of managers, risk (or uncertainty) is principally seen as an input to the strategy-making process. For instance, within the very influential "Resource-Based View" (Barney (1991)), uncertainty about the future complicates the process of deciding which "resources" to acquire and how to bundle them into "capabilities". Ultimately, this uncertainty results in some organisations achieving a sustained competitive advantage, whilst others do not. In another approach to strategy, "Real-Options Theory" (Dixit and Pindyck (1995)), it is precisely uncertainty about the future that makes the opportunity to defer investment decisions valuable. By contrast, the finance literature, both academic and practitioner, tends to focus solely on the perspective of (well-diversified) investors. In this context, the primary risk is the covariance of firm performance with the performance of the market in general (see discussion in Chapter 1), which is a consequence of the strategy adopted (primarily which industry sectors to operate in) by the managers of firms in the pursuit of profit.

I have consciously avoided the term "strategic risks" up to now, as it is widely misused, preferring instead to use Merton's (2005) term "value-adding risks". But the former expression does neatly capture the idea that some risks arise directly out of the strategic decisions that the organisation's managers take. I have also stressed throughout the book that decisions about risk management (primarily concerned with passive risks) and risk-taking (primarily concerned with value-adding risks) should be aligned. The discussion of risk treatment in Chapter 6 points to how strategy and risk, or, to be more precise, the activities of strategy-making and risk management, interact in practical terms. The logical extension of the bootstrapping approach taken in Chapter 6 is that both strategy decisions and risk management decisions should be based on consideration of a single overall quantitative model of profit and loss. Pursuing this approach, considerations of risk (and risk treatments) are indeed an important input to the strategy-making process: for example, the availability of cost-effective treatments for passive risks enables an organisation to take on additional value-adding risks. But strategy is also an important input to risk (treatment) decisions: the value of treating passive risks at any particular point in time is largely determined by the value that can be created by taking on additional value-adding risks at that time.

In the context of setting and implementing strategy, it is worth also briefly mentioning corporate governance. As discussed at various points throughout this book, the whole organisational attitude towards risk management, and alignment between risk management and risk taking, is shaped by senior management incentives. Whilst I have downplayed corporate governance throughout the discussion thus far, constructing appropriate remuneration packages for senior managers, in order to align their interests with those of other stakeholder groups, is a critical governance task for directors/trustees. If the structure of executive compensation packages protects the interests of key stakeholder groups, then directors should not need to devote excessive time and effort to monitoring the day-to-day actions of managers. This applies just as much to decisions about risk management as it does to any other strategic choices that executives make.

Where Does Risk Management Belong in the Organisation?

Some years ago, I was attacked (verbally) after giving a presentation on some research that I had conducted on the employment of risk management professionals at an Institute of Risk Management seminar. I was accused of wilfully perpetuating the nonsense that risk management must be a distinct function within the organisation, as opposed to being an integral part of everybody's job. I suspect that my accuser hadn't actually listened very carefully to what I had said. Nevertheless, he did raise an important question, which I have encountered in many different forms in the years since: should risk management be a separate function, and, if so, where does it belong in the organisation?

I have not specifically addressed this question so far, but I have dropped some hints in previous chapters. A central theme throughout the book is that risks should be aggregated across the whole organisation, and that decisions about risk management and risk-taking should be taken in a consistent manner. However, that is not the same as saying that there must be a single person or team responsible for risk management within the organisation: the idea of everybody taking some ownership and responsibility is conceptually attractive (although potentially hard to achieve in practice). Having repeatedly challenged the conflation of risk management and compliance, I would argue that responsibility should *not* sit within the compliance function. Beyond that I would suggest that (almost) any structure can work if people want it to (and, equally, no structure will work if people don't). Fundamentally, the line management of the people involved in risk management is less important than getting the risk management framework (see Chapters 3 and 4) right in the first place, and ensuring that the organisation has the necessary capabilities. The specific capabilities required to implement the approach outlined in this book can be created through many different combinations of permanent, in-house risk management staff, temporary secondment of staff with relevant data analysis skills from other areas of the organisation and the judicious use of contractors and consultants.

Crises and Black-Swans

I first touched on the subject of the rarest and most extreme events in Chapter 1, and this issue has reappeared frequently in the remaining chapters. In Chapter 2, I reviewed the evidence that personal experience or awareness of such crises influences decisions on risk management, in Chapter 5, I considered how extreme events can be captured in quantitative models and in Chapter 7, I looked at some evidence on the mitigating effect of risk management activities when organisations experience a crisis.

The practical approach taken throughout this book has been to explicitly acknowledge that one cannot possibly hope to identify, much less quantify, all events that may occur in the future. It is important to reiterate in this context that my purpose has never been to calculate precise probabilities of particular levels of extreme losses. It is also important to reiterate that:

- The recommended approach to risk identification and analysis (see Chapter 5), based on the impact on the organisation not the precise trigger event; and
- The skewed distributions used to model the impacts of these risks (including lognormal, power-law and extreme value theorem)

already allow for the possibility of occasional extreme events.

Fundamentally though, the key point is that, in almost all cases, there is a natural limit to the maximum possible impact on each stakeholder group. The concept of limited liability allows investors to cap their liabilities at the amount that they have invested in the firm. Even if an entrepreneurial owner has not taken advantage of this risk mitigation, their losses are essentially capped at their own personal wealth, beyond which they become personally bankrupt. Likewise, lenders can generally only lose the amount that they have loaned to the organisation, and managers and other staff members can only lose their job once. As was famously demonstrated in the credit crunch, it is very difficult to claw back bonus payments already made to senior managers, even if the firm subsequently goes bust. Thus whilst, in theory, a risk with a very low probability but extremely high impact could greatly affect estimates of expected outcome and variability of outcomes in the overall profit and loss distribution, in practice it cannot because the impact on each stakeholder group is limited.*

That said, I would strongly advise organisations to prioritise investment in developing a crisis management capability

---

* This is, of course, different in the financial services sector, where the interconnectedness of banks means that the failure of a single firm can have a systemic impact way beyond the loss of its entire value.

within their overall risk management programme. As acknowledged in Chapter 7, empirical evidence on the efficacy of
these approaches is still inconclusive, but all of my professional experience leads me to strongly believe that a flexible
ability to manage disruptions in whatever form they emerge is
one of the most effective components of any risk management
programme. This includes, of course, being able to communicate effectively during an incident (see Crisis Communications
sidebar).

CRISIS COMMUNICATIONS CASE STUDY SIDEBAR

The fast-food company KFC has been operating in the
United Kingdom since 1965, and by 2018 had around 900
outlets. It is 95% owned and operated by franchisees,
who typically own and operate a number of sites. On 14
February 2018, KFC moved to a new logistics partner, and
by 18 February most of KFC's UK outlets had had to close
as they had run out of chicken. Unsurprisingly, there was
widespread coverage of the situation on social media, both
from angry customers and "expert" commentators.

KFC responded in kind, with initial communication via
social media within hours. These communications clearly
took responsibility for the situation, focusing on what had
gone wrong, how it was being resolved and when it would
be fixed. The social media posts were phrased in straightforward language and made judicious use of humour. KFC
also responded promptly to customer questions posted
on social media. This was followed up by a major communication campaign across social and traditional media,
including national newspaper adverts. The "FCK" campaign focused on apologising to customers and thanking
staff and franchisees, but, once again, was infused with
humour. Crucially, KFC resisted the temptation to try and

pass the blame onto others. By 23 February, 700 outlets had successfully reopened and, in due course, the "FCK" campaign won multiple PR industry awards!

KFC's response is widely regarded in the industry as a "masterclass" in crisis communications, but most of the commentary on the incident focuses on the skilful crafting of a message that aligned with their brand and resonated with their core market. Whilst this was undoubtedly important, I would argue that practical communications considerations were equally important. The communications response could only be implemented successfully because KFC had an experienced in-house communications team, who were already used to working closely with the two PR agencies who supported them during the incident. At a practical level, this meant that they were able to handle six months' worth of media enquiries in a single week. Another practical aspect, as noted above, is that social media queries from customers were being handled in a timely fashion. Once again, this had to be planned and resourced in advance, for example, who is responsible for monitoring social media and who is able to post on social media channels?

Without detracting from the positive aspects of KFC's response, it is worth noting that the company was fortunate in that the specific nature of the incident did not generate a huge volume of incoming calls from customers. Handling incoming calls is a core component of crisis communications, and there are numerous recent examples where this has not been handled well, including a series of high-profile IT outages within the UK financial services sector. Despite having tens of thousands of directly employed staff, and an enormous network of branches, banks have repeatedly appeared unable to communicate effectively with customers when faced with disruption.

In conclusion, it is also important to highlight that the communication response only worked because KFC was able to swiftly resolve the operational issues. I suspect that customers would rapidly have become less impressed with the flow of humorous communications if the disruption had persisted for a second and third week. Ultimately, crisis communication is only ever part of an overall crisis management response.

Applicability to the Public and Not-for-Profit Sectors

As acknowledged in the Introduction, much of the research evidence discussed throughout this book has been based on studies of commercial firms; this does beg the question of to what extent any findings can be generalised to public bodies and not-for-profit organisations. Clearly, there are some practical limits to what can be applied outside of the sphere of quoted companies but, I would argue, the general principles still apply. Indeed, the need to understand and accommodate the different risk perspectives of a diverse network of stakeholder groups is particularly acute in the public and not-for-profit sectors.

Whilst it seems nonsensical to suggest that public sector organisations are not engaging with risk management – seemingly all surveys indicate that they are more likely to adopt formal risk management approaches than private sector organisations – it is the focus of many risk management programmes that I would question. Public bodies often manifest the most extreme examples of the compliance approach to risk management, first highlighted in the Introduction. Sadly, I have repeatedly encountered the attitude that the maintenance of a detailed (but entirely qualitative) risk register, and associated "heat-map", is an end in itself, rather than the beginning of a search for more data and a hunt for cost-effective risk treatments.

Absent a meaningful definition of "owners", and a profit motive, the value-creating benefits of risk management appear to have been widely neglected outside of the commercial sphere. But, as argued in Chapter 2, the potential for risk management interventions to improve expected outcomes, to reduce the likelihood of extreme events (financial and non-financial) and to reduce variability in outcomes is valuable to all organisations. The need to focus on, and measure, return on investment will only increase as the public sector continues to cope with very limited resources and adopts more commercial ways of operating. It is very much hoped that this book will stimulate more positive thinking on risk management in the public and not-for-profit sectors, and the wider adoption of quantitative approaches.

An alternative example of risk analysis and treatment, specifically applicable to the public and not-for-profit sectors, is provided in Annex C.

Would Any of This Have Made a Difference in the Covid-19 Pandemic?

In the current environment, it is perfectly legitimate to ask whether any of what I have proposed in previous chapters would have made a difference to our ability to deal with the significant challenges presented by Covid-19. I shall look at this question at various different levels.

As I have already discussed, the risk of a pandemic had been acknowledged at the national level for many years; indeed, it was highlighted as the most significant risk on the *UK National Risk Register*. However, the format of the *National*

Risk Register does not provide any mechanism for calculating what would be a reasonable amount to invest in mitigating this risk, despite all the necessary data being available. It would have been perfectly possible to construct likelihood and impact distributions for pandemics using historical data from the United Kingdom and the output from the most up-to-date epidemiological models. Indeed, the Head of Emergency Preparedness for the NHS was quoted prior to the 2009 flu pandemic in Martin (2008, p.20) as saying:

> The worst-case scenario, a flu pandemic in the UK similar to the 1918 pandemic would infect 24-30 million people and leave close to 1 million dead.

Historical UK data could have been augmented by data from countries affected by more recent outbreaks such as SARS and MERS: this search for external data might well have had the additional benefit of highlighting the importance of "track and trace" systems and other novel (from a UK perspective) approaches to managing pandemics. Such a quantitative approach at the national level would, most probably, have justified the commitment of greater resources to planning and preparing for a pandemic. Moreover, resources would have been focused on mitigation measures that had been proven to work in previous pandemics elsewhere.

Turning now to the level of individual organisations, which is, after all, the focus of this book. Absent updated pandemic modelling from the UK government, organisations could have reverted to existing flu pandemic guidance, looked at data from counties affected by SARS and MERS outbreaks and/ or purchased commercial modelling data to inform their risk assessments. Even just using the UK government's flu pandemic guidance, which was widely available prior to 2009, would have provided a solid basis for planning. For example, it predicted that:

- It would take less than a month from the first global reports of a new flu virus for first cases to reach the United Kingdom;
- There would be one or more pandemic waves of three to four months duration, with up to 25% of the population becoming ill in each wave; and
- Absence rates would peak at 15-20% in each wave (including those that are ill, those caring for sick relatives and parents who cannot attend work because schools are closed).

Whilst Covid-19 has behaved very differently to flu from an epidemiological perspective, a risk assessment based on these guidelines would have captured many of the operational impacts that were experienced at an organisational level, and contingency plans based on these figures would have been relatively effective in 2020. It would, of course, have been much harder to model the enormous, and sector-specific, impact on demand of effectively shutting down large parts of the economy for extended periods.

Finally, I should like to share a personal perspective on how Covid-19 has affected our own firm. The key operational risk to a micro business like ours is the loss of one (or both) of the two principals, and we partially mitigate this risk through the purchase of life and critical illness insurance. Compared to this, operational risks related to loss of premises or IT are relatively unimportant and easily mitigated. The key financial risk is non-payment by a customer, which we manage in a number of ways, and, so far, have not sustained a single loss. So, entering the pandemic, the key risk to the business was actually variability in demand for our services. Our expected revenues for 2020 can be estimated from a simple (ordinary least squares) regression analysis of our revenues over the 11 years that we had been in business up to and including 2019 (Figure 8.1).

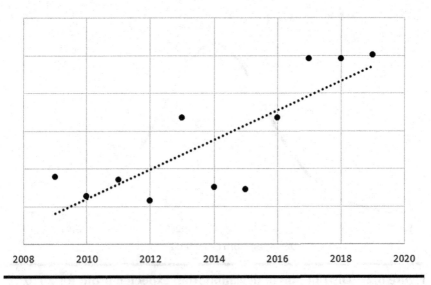

Figure 8.1   Annual revenues 2009-2019

However, given the wide spread of data-points on either side of the best-fit-line, there is considerable uncertainty in what the actual revenue (and hence profit) will be for 2020. A modelled distribution of the deviation from the expected profit for 2020 is shown in Figure 8.2.

On this basis, there is roughly a 5% chance of a shortfall of more than £40,000 and a 1% chance of a shortfall of over £75,000 from the expected profit in 2020. Risk management, in the sense discussed in this book, is largely irrelevant to mitigating risks such as these. All one can really do is to ensure that the business model is flexible enough to weather reasonably foreseeable downturns over a sensible timescale; in this case, a shortfall of £40,000 (representing a once-in-20-years event) might be a sensible basis for planning.* As it happened, a fall in demand was indeed the major impact of Covid-19 on our business, although the actual downturn in

---

* Holding cash reserves may be part of that flexibility: one could calculate the cost of maintaining different levels of reserves versus the estimated cost of experiencing financial distress to work out an optimum.

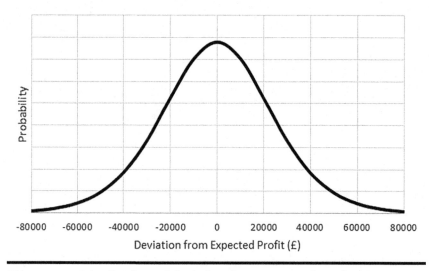

Figure 8.2 Distribution of deviation from expected profit for 2020

revenues was just over £50,000, close to the third percentile of the distribution (so this was more like a once-in-30-years event). Thus, absent assistance from the UK government and/ or personal savings, we could well have experienced real difficulties.

So, I would argue, quantitative risk management could have made a significant improvement to how both governments and individual organisations prepared and planned for a pandemic, even without knowing the precise epidemiological details of Covid-19 in advance. That said, there could still have been enormous damage to the economy, and many organisations would still have experienced financial distress. As I have argued throughout this book, organisations (and governments) should make judgements about risk management based on return on investment, and there comes a point at which reducing risk any further is no longer cost-effective. For some organisations, the cost of mitigating the impact of Covid-19 would simply not have been worthwhile: failure of these organisations does not in any way imply a failure of risk management. It seems perverse to say, but occasional failures actually constitute positive evidence, that risks are being managed appropriately. I am reminded in this context of the public outcry some years ago when, in the midst of severe winter weather in the United Kingdom, many local authorities ran out of rock salt to treat the road network. Amidst the many voices arguing that they should hold greater stocks of salt (it was never stated exactly how much greater), I took the more positive view that running out once in my lifetime was possibly evidence of a sensible cost-benefit analysis: the impact of very occasionally running out was probably less than the ongoing costs of holding vastly increased stocks.

Summary of Key Ideas

Know Your Organisation's Stakeholders

The central theme of this book is that, when thinking about risk, it is important to ask the question "risk to whom?" Even relatively small organisations have a complex network of stakeholders, and different stakeholder groups may be impacted very differently by the same event. It is important to understand, and take account of, these different risk perspectives in implementing a risk management programme.

Risk Assessment Is Not an End in Itself

Another important theme is that the identification and analysis of risks is not an end in itself, but part of the overall risk management process. A simple, quantitative approach to risk management has been proposed, which attempts to rebalance the risk management process towards affording equal emphasis to searching for and evaluating risk treatments.

Data

The entire approach to risk management proposed in this book is data-driven, as well as using internal data, the judicious use of data from outside the organisation is always to be encouraged. However, an initial (perceived) lack of data should be no barrier to beginning the process. Crucially, the risk analysis process should identify where the value of additional information is greatest, and thereby drive an ongoing, targeted search for more data.

The Role of Standards and "Good Practice"

The development of the paradigm of integrated risk management/strategic risk management/enterprise risk management in recent decades was discussed in Chapter 3. In particular, I looked critically at one widely adopted approach to integrated risk management: ISO 31000. There is much useful advice in the ISO standard, and my proposed approach incorporates many ideas from it, particularly around the need for clear roles and responsibilities and effective communication with different stakeholder groups. However, the approach that I propose in Chapters 4-6 deviates from ISO 31000 in some important respects. In particular, I strongly believe that its strict delineation between risk assessment and risk treatment leads to a focus on the risks themselves, rather than on exploring possible risk treatments.

Granularity of Risks

One of the central practical challenges in risk management is how much to aggregate or decompose risks; over the years, I have seen a vast range of opinions on this. At one extreme I have encountered small organisations that have captured hundreds of risks; at the other extreme, there are much larger organisations that have only a dozen or so aggregated risks at the corporate level. Indeed, one client insisted that there can only ever be a maximum of ten risks on their risk register! I cannot give a simple rule-of-thumb for how many risks you should have per 100 employees (or million pounds of revenue). However, I was able to give some practical advice in Chapter 5. When embarking on the risk identification process, I advise describing risks in terms of the impact on the organisation (or, more precisely, on the organisation's stakeholders) rather than the specific trigger event or scenario. However, during the risk analysis phase, some of these risks may need to be disaggregated because it becomes clear that they are not drawn from the same population.

Managing Conflict and Tensions

Differing stakeholder perspectives may lead to conflict and tension which impedes the implementation of risk management. One of the ways in which organisations "resolve" these conflicts is through delegating some decision-making to a lower level. Just as senior management incentives should be aligned with stakeholders' risk perspectives, middle managers should be incentivised to ensure that departmental decisions are based on the agreed organisational risk appetite rather than a local (or personal) risk appetite. Crucially, this may require a shift towards rewarding people for following appropriate decision-making processes, rather than rewards based on the short-term outcomes of those decisions. Organisations also "resolve" conflicts by attending to different goals sequentially, so the focus of a risk management programme may evolve over time as it seeks to address different stakeholders' concerns.

References

Barney J, 1991, Firm Resources and Sustained Competitive Advantage, *Journal of Management*, 17(1): 99–120.

Dixit A and Pindyck R, 1995, The Options Approach to Capital Investment, *Harvard Business Review*, 73(3): 105–115.

Hubbard D, 2020, *The Failure of Risk Management: Why it's Broken and How to Fix It*, 2nd Edition, Hoboken, NJ: Wiley.

ISO, 2009, *ISO 31000: Risk Management - Guidance and Best Practice*, Geneva: International Organization for Standardization.

Martin D, 2008, *Managing Risk in Extreme Environments: Front-Line Business Lessons for Corporate and Financial Institutions*, London: Kogan Page.

Merton R, 2005, You Have More Capital Than You Think, *Harvard Business Review*, 83(11): 84–94.

Appendix A:
Risk Return Relationships in UK Listed Companies

Chapter 1 explained why variability in outcomes was unattractive to the owners (usually shareholders) of firms; I also argued that, as well as acting in the interests of shareholders, senior managers had their own personal reasons to wish to minimise such variability. Chapter 2 examined some empirical evidence from the stock market showing a positive relationship between variability in returns and the returns themselves, suggesting that investors required compensation for accepting this variability. One would expect to find a similar, positive, relationship between accounting-based measures of risk and performance, reflecting managers' requirements to be compensated for accepting variability. However, as explained in Chapter 2, the empirical evidence for this relationship has been inconclusive.

Ever since Bowman's (1980) finding that accounting-based measures of risk and performance at the firm level were *negatively* related, there has been significant interest in analysing such risk-return relationships and numerous empirical studies have been published. However, these studies, using a number of different methods and data from different periods of time, have produced divergent and often contradictory results. The study summarised here (Roberts (2016, Chapter 5)) contains full details, based on a large sample of UK listed firms, seeks to address the limitations identified in previous studies by:

- Using a more complete range of risk measures;
- Including a greater range of control variables;
- Removing firm fixed effects (to allow for the fact that some firms may just be better managed than others); and
- Using a range of different statistical techniques to deal with the problem of extreme outlying values.

Data

The analysis uses risk measures estimated over five overlapping five-year time periods from 2003-2007 to 2007-2011: it is important to highlight that this timeframe includes the global financial crisis (or "credit crunch"), beginning in 2007. Performance is measured in the year following the end of each five-year estimation period (i.e. 2008, 2009, 2010, 2011 and 2012). Because of issues with the availability of data, there are different numbers of firms included in each time period, varying approximately between 600 and 1000. Accounting data were obtained from the FAME database and market data from Datastream.

The dependent variable (representing performance) is return on equity (ROE), defined as profit before tax divided by the *market* value of equity. The following three risk measures were included as explanatory variables, all estimated over a five-year period:

- Standard deviation of return on assets (SD of ROA);
- Covariance of returns with the market (Beta); and

▪ Standard deviation of cashflow (SD of cashflow).

The principal focus of the study is the relationship between SD of ROA over a five-year estimation period and ROE in the year following the end of that estimation period. Two control variables were also included, as these might have an effect on performance:

▪ Size of the firm, defined as the natural log of turnover; and
▪ Market power of the firm, defined as turnover of the firm divided by the total turnover for that industry sector.

Finally, a dummy variable for high performance was included, in case prior performance influenced the risk perspectives of stakeholders. This was set to "1" if firm ROE over the five-year period was above the median value. Summary statistics for the pooled sample are shown in Table A.1.

In order to remove firm fixed effects (such as better management), all variables were "first-differenced". That is, the previous period's value was subtracted from each variable before any regressions were conducted. There are therefore only four periods of analysis in the study, designated by the year in which performance was measured: 2009, 2010, 2011 and 2012.

Table A.1 Summary Statistics for the Pooled Sample of Data

	N	Mean	Median	Min	Max	SD
ROE	3,953	-0.0915	0.0568	-125	11.7	2.18
Size	3,953	10.8	10.6	1.39	19.3	2.86
Power	3,938	0.00338	0.0000898	4.24×10^9	0.240	0.0145
SD of ROA	3,953	0.134	0.0667	0.000453	3.91	0.252
Beta	3,953	0.625	0.569	-2.45	4.87	0.434
SD of cashflow	3,953	0.0860	0.0519	.0000205	1.27	0.111

Results

All analysis was conducted in STATA. Various different regression techniques were used to deal with the extreme outlying values present in the dataset. Results are reported in Table A.2 for M-estimator regression.*

The key finding is that the parameter estimate for SD of ROA is statistically significant in all but one time period but, crucially, varies between positive and negative values. It is also interesting to note the significant parameter estimates for the interaction term between High Performance and SD of ROA in both 2009 and 2012. This is presented in a slightly different way in Table A.3, by combining the parameter estimates for SD of ROA and the interaction term between High Performance and SD of ROA.

So whilst, in the first period in the study, there was a *positive* relationship between risk (SD of ROA) and subsequent performance (ROE) for all firms, in the final period of the study, the effect was much reduced for high-performing firms, and the relationship was actually *negative* for low-performing firms.

Discussion

The main finding from this study was that, in common with the empirical evidence from stock market data considered in Chapter 2, the relationship between accounting measures of risk and return appears to be highly dependent on prevailing economic conditions. In the relatively benign economic environment that existed prior to the credit crunch, managers were

---

* The M-estimator regression is designed to reduce the influence of extreme outliers rather than simply deleting them. This is important in risk research as much important information is contained in these extremes. The results using other robust regression techniques were very similar.

Table A.2 M-Estimator Regression Results, Dependent Variable ROE 2009-2012

	ROE in 2012	ROE in 2011	ROE in 2010	ROE in 2009
Size	–0.016**	–0.006	0.020	–0.238**
	(–2.58)	(–0.84)	(0.92)	(–2.77)
Power	–1.097	0.677	–0.915	2.461
	(–1.06)	(0.74)	(–0.42)	(0.45)
SD of ROA	–0.121***	0.068*	0.438***	4.755***
	(–6.81)	(2.36)	(11.61)	(41.71)
Beta	–0.067**	0.047*	0.029	–0.126***
	(–2.79)	(2.57)	(1.43)	(–3.33)
SD of cashflow	–0.056+	–0.090*	0.091	–0.007
	(–1.93)	(–2.07)	(1.09)	(–0.04)
High performance * SD of ROA	0.314***	0.118	0.387+	–1.877***
	(5.98)	(0.99)	(1.91)	(–6.37)
Constant	–0.011***	0.009***	0.001	0.022
	(–5.85)	(4.48)	(0.18)	(1.47)
R^2	0.08	0.02	0.19	0.78
N	884	775	668	554

t-statistics are shown in parentheses.
Significance levels are indicated as follows: + $p < 0.1$, * $p < 0.05$, ** $p < 0.01$, ***$p < 0.001$.

generally achieving a significant increase in ROE in return for taking risk. An absolute increase of 1% in SD of ROA (compared to a median SD of ROA of 6.5% in 2009) leads to a predicted absolute increase in ROE of between 3% and 5% (compared to a median ROE of 7% in 2009).

Table A.3   Relationship between ROE and SD of ROA for Low and High-Performing Firms, 2009 and 2012

	ROE in 2012	*ROE in 2009*
Low-performing firms	−0.121***	4.755***
High-performing firms	0.193***	2.878***

*** Significance level p < 0.001

However, in the much more difficult environment in the final period of the study following the financial crisis, it appears that managers were willing to accept much lower expected compensation for taking risk. Indeed, in low-performing firms, the risk premium was actually negative in this period, implying a willingness to exploit any potential opportunities, even if the benefits were not clear. On the basis of this study, I can only speculate whether this really reflected the interests (at that time) of shareholders, or whether it was driven by managerial self-preservation.

These findings reinforce the importance of reviewing risk criteria regularly, with all stakeholder groups, in light of changes to the environment in which the organisation operates. A bootstrapping approach to implementing this in practice is explained in Chapter 6.

References

Bowman E, 1980, A Risk/Return Paradox for Strategic Management, *Sloan Management Review*, 21(3): 17–31.

Roberts P, 2016, Measuring and Managing Risk in UK Listed Firms, PhD thesis, University of Nottingham.

Appendix B:
The Impact of Covid-19 on FTSE 100 Share Prices

As well as being a terrible human tragedy, and triggering a global economic crisis, the Covid-19 outbreak provided a unique opportunity to study how different businesses manage disruption, and which approaches are most effective. Specifically, this study looks at whether large firms that have adopted good practice in business continuity management (BCM) suffered less impact on their share prices during the Covid-19 outbreak than those that haven't.

The Covid-19 pandemic is fundamentally different to most disruptions in that all firms were impacted simultaneously. Therefore, instead of the usual practice of comparing changes in the share price of one or more affected firms relative to the rest of the market (known as an "event study"), this study is a straightforward (ordinary-least-squares) regression of the changes in each firm's share price at various points in time against a range of explanatory and control variables.

In late February 2020, share prices around the world began a sharp decline. The FTSE 100 index, having been relatively stable between 7,100 and 7,700 for the previous six months, fell from 7,457 at the close on 19 February to 4,994.90 at the close on 23 March. Clearly, against this overall decline, different firms' share prices were affected to a greater or lesser extent, depending on both the nature of their business and, presumably, the steps that they took to respond to the crisis.

The hypothesis that is tested here is that firms that have adopted good practice in BCM, proxied by their employment of one or more members of the Business Continuity Institute (BCI), will tend to respond more effectively to the crisis, and that this will be reflected in a lower impact on their share prices. Even if firms' BCM programmes have not included specific pandemic planning, it should be expected that sound generic BCM strategies (e.g. tried and tested procedures for communicating with staff and customers and a process for monitoring and responding to disruption in supply chains) would enable firms that have adopted good practice in BCM to outperform rivals in responding to Covid-19.

Data

The study looks at the share prices of firms in the FTSE 100 (as of 18th March 2020) at 4-week intervals over a period of 52 weeks from 17 February 2020 to 15 February 2021. Adjusted closing share prices were downloaded from Yahoo Finance on 17 February 2022. The analysis was restricted to the FTSE 100 for two reasons:

- The practical difficulties of manually collecting data for a larger sample; and
- The concern that using the employment of BCI members as a proxy for adopting good practice loses its validity with smaller firms, as they may well utilise contractors and consultants to implement BCM.

However, this small sample size does have implications for the ability of the study to detect small effect sizes: this will be discussed further in the final section. Six firms were excluded from the analysis because some required data were not available, leaving a total of 94 firms. The restriction of the sample to large firms also means that any findings cannot necessarily be generalised to other types of organisations.

There is a single explanatory variable in the regression analysis: employment of at least one member of the BCI. A search of the "Community" database on the BCI website (on 8 April 2020) identified 19 firms in the FTSE 100 that employed at least one BCI member. It should be noted that this is almost certainly an underestimate, given that not all BCI members have entered their details into the database.[*]

A number of control variables were included in the regression in an attempt to control for differential impacts on share prices due to the different natures of firms' businesses.

■ Beta is a measure of how returns from an individual firm co-vary with the market as a whole over time. Whilst this long-term relationship may not strictly apply in a crisis, it is still important to include the possibility of some degree of this normal covariance in the model. Beta values for each firm, calculated over the preceding five years, were downloaded from Yahoo Finance on 20 March 2020.

■ Debt Ratio was included as a measure of financial leverage. Firms that were highly leveraged would be less able to access additional debt finance to deal with the consequences of Covid-19, and more likely to experience financial distress as revenues fell. Debt Ratio was calculated by dividing long-term debt by long-term debt plus equity.[†]

---

[*] The BCI provided the author with a full membership list for a previous study in 2011, which identified that 32 firms in the FTSE 100 employed at least one BCI member at that time.

[†] Long-term debt is the sum of ADVFN fields "Creditors long", "Creditors others", "Subordinated loans" and "Insurance funds; equity is the sum of ADVFN fields "Ordinary capital & reserves" and "Preferences & minorities".

Table B.1 Summary Statistics for Control Variables

	Mean	Min	Max	Standard Deviation
Beta	0.70	-0.49	2.0	0.40
Debt ratio	51.4%	0.2%	156%	28.7%
Liquidity	12.2%	-22.7%	76.1%	21.0%

All data were taken from the ADVFN website for the last
financial year end prior to the start of the study period.
■ Liquidity was also included, as firms that lacked liquidity
were more likely to experience financial distress as their
cashflow was impacted by Covid-19. Liquidity was calculated by subtracting current liabilities from current assets
and dividing the result by the total assets.* All data were
taken from ADVFN for the last financial year end prior to
the start of the study period.

Summary statistics for these control variables are shown in
Table B.1.

Dummy variables were also included for three specific
industry sectors: travel and leisure (6 firms), pharmaceuticals
(4 firms) and financial services (17 firms). The travel industry
was extremely badly hit by suspension of international travel
and, subsequently, restrictions on domestic activities, so it is
expected that share prices of these firms would be particularly
badly hit. By contrast, pharmaceutical firms had a critical role
in the response to the Covid-19 outbreak, so it is expected
that their share prices would be less badly affected than other
firms. No specific predictions are made about any sector-
specific impact on financial services, but employment of BCI
members is disproportionately high in the industry. There is

---

* Current assets is the sum of ADVFN fields "Cash & securities", "Debtors",
"Stocks" and "Current assets – other"; current liabilities is the ADVFN field
"Creditors – short".

therefore the danger that any impact specific to financial services might erroneously be associated with adoption of BCM good practice if there is not a specific dummy variable for the sector.

Results

All regression analyses were performed using STATA; results for each time period are shown in Table B.2.

In the early stages of the pandemic (up to and including week 24), much of the observed cross-sectional variation in changes to share price can be accounted for by beta and the industry dummies. In particular:

- As predicted, there was a negative association between beta and share prices (statistically significant in every period);
- As predicted, there was a positive association between the pharmaceutical sector dummy and share prices (statistically significant in every period); and
- As predicted, there was a negative association between the travel and leisure sector dummy and share prices (statistically significant in every period).

With the single exception of week 24, the regression found no statistically significant association between share prices and the financial services dummy, DBVE or liquidity.

As the pandemic continued though, the pattern changed, with the associations between beta and share prices becoming insignificant after week 24, and the association between the pharmaceutical sector dummy and share prices becoming insignificant after week 28. (The negative association between the travel and leisure sector dummy and share prices remained significant throughout.) Most importantly though, there was a

Table B.2 OLS Regression Results, Dependent Variable Change in Share Price

	Week 4	Week 8	Week 12	Week 16	Week 20	Week 24	Week 28
BCI	0.00153	-0.0450	-0.0587+	-0.0616+	-0.0605	-0.0952*	-0.108*
	(-0.05)	(-1.53)	(-1.70)	(-1.96)	(-1.60)	(-2.15)	(-2.33)
Beta	-0.134***	-0.169***	-0.166*	-0.103+	-0.113+	-0.151+	-0.114
	(-3.63)	(-3.69)	(-2.53)	(-1.80)	(-1.85)	(-1.87)	(-1.42)
Travel & Leisure	-0.219***	-0.241***	-0.315***	-0.258***	-0.323***	-0.364***	-0.307**
	(-5.34)	(-3.73)	(-4.19)	(-3.84)	(-4.02)	(-3.68)	(-3.02)
Pharma	0.163***	0.215***	0.253***	0.212***	0.185***	0.185**	0.157*
	(4.21)	(4.38)	(3.78)	(5.20)	(4.43)	(3.36)	(2.22)
Financial Services	0.0358	0.0607	0.0666	0.0589	0.0719	0.114+	0.0581
	(0.93)	(1.46)	(1.28)	(1.33)	(1.42)	(1.88)	(0.91)
DBVE	0.00009	-0.000491	-0.000575	-0.000633	-0.000920	-0.00134	-0.00103
	(0.19)	(-0.68)	(-0.69)	(-0.88)	(-1.02)	(-1.25)	(-0.90)
Liquidity	-0.000433	-0.000777	-0.000684	-0.000844	-0.000582	-0.00147	-0.000952
	(-0.63)	(-1.08)	(-0.80)	(-1.15)	(-0.69)	(-1.37)	(-0.88)
Constant	-0.229***	-0.0823+	-0.0661	-0.0410	-0.0134	0.0687	0.0136
	(-7.10)	(-1.95)	(-1.18)	(-0.86)	(-0.25)	(1.01)	(0.20)
N	94	94	94	94	94	94	94

(Continued)

Table B.2 (Continued)   OLS Regression Results, Dependent Variable Change in Share Price

	Week 32	Week 36	Week 40	Week 44	Week 48	Week 52
BCI	-0.126*	-0.126*	-0.110**	-0.118**	-0.128***	-0.149**
	(-2.35)	(-2.50)	(-2.77)	(-2.73)	(-2.66)	(-2.94)
Beta	-0.109	-0.113	-0.0342	0.00569	0.0604	0.0947
	(-1.23)	(-1.41)	(-0.46)	(0.07)	(0.59)	(0.85)
Travel & Leisure	-0.452***	-0.414***	-0.334**	-0.421***	-0.513***	-0.494**
	(-3.71)	(-3.83)	(-3.05)	(-3.69)	(-3.86)	(-3.45)
Pharma	0.130	0.0886	0.0812	-0.0143	0.00894	-0.0441
	(1.34)	(0.86)	(0.80)	(-0.14)	(0.09)	(-0.50)
Financial Services	0.0702	0.0572	0.0360	0.0210	-0.0108	0.0103
	(0.90)	(0.78)	(0.55)	(0.30)	(-0.14)	(0.12)
DBVE	-0.00150	-0.000990	-0.000620	-0.000783	-0.000777	-0.000618
	(-1.07)	(-0.79)	(-0.55)	(-0.64)	(-0.58)	(-0.44)
Liquidity	-0.00144	-0.00109	-0.000237	-0.000173	-0.000420	0.000139
	(-1.18)	(-0.94)	(-0.25)	(-0.16)	(-0.33)	(0.11)
Constant	0.0751	0.00852	0.0232	0.0593	0.0582	0.0347
	(0.96)	(0.11)	(0.31)	(0.70)	(0.65)	(0.37)
N	94	94	94	94	94	94

t-statistics are shown in parentheses.
Significance levels are indicated as follows: + p < .1, * p < .05, ** p < .01, *** p < .001.

significant *negative* association between employment of a BCI member and share prices from week 24 onwards: by the end of the study period this accounted for a difference of 14.9% in firm value.

By way of an illustration, the evolution of the share price of a hypothetical baseline firm with beta = 1 over the period of the study is illustrated in Figure B.1. For comparison, the graph also shows the share price for three other types of firms over the period (beta = 1 in all cases).

- A firm in the travel and leisure sector;
- A firm in the pharmaceuticals sector; and
- A firm that employs one or more members of the BCI.

Discussion

The study fails to find any support for the hypothesis that adopting BCM good practice, as proxied by the employment of one or more BCI members, positively affected changes

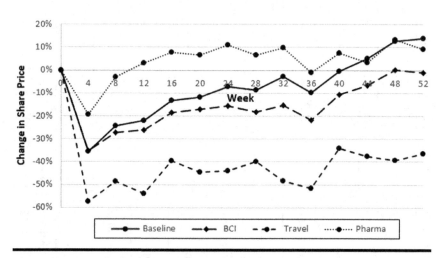

Figure B.1   Evolution of share prices February 2020 to February 2021

in share prices during the Covid-19 pandemic. Indeed, for a significant period during the study there is a statistically significant, *negative* association with share prices. As mentioned previously, the small sample size limits the power of the regression. It would have been entirely unsurprising for the study to be inconclusive, but the finding of a significant positive effect was truly shocking. I consider below some possible explanations.

It could be that investors had already factored in the superior risk management capabilities of firms that employ a BCI member into their share prices. As I discussed in Chapter 1, even well-diversified investors benefit from reducing variability in performance,* so investors may pay a premium for shares in firms that can manage risk more effectively. If that is the case, then some of the observed negative effect could simply be a "correction": the share prices of firms that had implemented BCM fell because there was no evidence that they performed any better than their peers in responding to the unprecedented challenges of the pandemic. However, this explanation seems unlikely as a complete explanation for two reasons:

■ The employment of BCI members is not generally publicly available information; and
■ The "premium" (over 10% of firm value) just seems too high.

Rabin and Bazerman (2019), which was discussed in Chapter 4, provide another possible explanation. Recalling their argument that managing everyday risks actually makes organisations less resilient because it uses up resources, it could be that many of the firms that have implemented BCM have utilised too much resource in mitigating everyday risks, thereby reducing the reserves they had available to them to cope with

---

* Some empirical studies were discussed in Chapter 4 too.

a major disruption like Covid-19. Indeed, one could extend
this line of reasoning further: even if the BCM activities undertaken will indeed provide a good return on investment in the
long term, they have still depleted resources for dealing with
the specific challenges of Covid-19 in the short term. However,
logically, at least some of this diminution in reserves should be
evident in reduced liquidity and/or increased leverage, both of
which were explicitly controlled for in the regression.

Given the inability of the previous two possible explanations to account for the magnitude of the observed results, it is
necessary to at least consider the possibility that firms that had
implemented BCM actually reacted less well operationally to the
challenges that they were presented with in 2020-2021. As discussed above, one would expect that generic elements of good
practice in BCM (such as robust command and control arrangements and good crisis communications procedures) would have
been of benefit even if firms hadn't specifically planned for a
pandemic, so the finding is highly counter-intuitive. However,
it is possible that pre-prepared plans for other forms of disruption (e.g. denial of access to premises) were inappropriately and
inflexibly applied in response to Covid-19, thereby destroying
value. However, once again, it seems highly implausible that
this could account for a 15% reduction in firm value.

Finally, the aim of risk management is not to reduce risk
per se, but to cost-effectively mitigate passive risks in order to
enable organisations to take on value-adding risks. It is therefore possible that firms that had successfully implemented
BCM took on additional value-adding risk, as they mitigated
their passive risks. Even though they may have been better
prepared to respond operationally, the increased value-adding
risk would have meant that these firms were particularly hard
hit by the shutting down of the economy during the pandemic. So, although these firms were very exposed to this
specific form of disruption, they may well prosper in the long
term. This is an interesting hypothesis; the challenge for future

research is to work out a way of testing it by somehow estimating firms' proportions of passive and value-adding risks from published accounting and market data.

I have suggested four possible explanations for the existence of a negative relationship between the adoption of good practice in BCM and firms' share prices during the Covid-19 pandemic. Whilst the final suggestion is certainly worthy of further study, it seems implausible that, even in aggregate, these four explanations can completely account for the size of the observed effect. Absent a definitive explanation, I offer this final case study primarily as an illustration of some of the complexities inherent in managing risk: it is certainly not intended to imply that the work of BCM professionals, of which I am one, is not of any value. Even if these firms' attempts to manage passive risks through BCM were highly effective, they are only part of an overall risk management approach, including an awareness of the value-adding risks that the organisation faces.

First and foremost, this case study highlights the possibility of risk management interventions not having the desired effect, and hence the need to constantly monitor the impact of risk treatments. I embarked on this study expecting that firms that had adopted good practice in BCM would perform better than their peers during the pandemic: it is only by actually measuring their performance that I now know that they didn't and can start to look for reasons why this is the case. The case study also illustrates that risk management is a long game: it may well be that the firms that had adopted good practice in BCM were doing the right thing for the long term, but there may still be significant setbacks in the short term.

Reference

Rabin M and Bazerman M, 2019, Fretting about Modest Risks is a Mistake, *California Management Review*, 61(3): 34–48.

Appendix C: Alternative Numerical Example

This appendix presents an alternative numerical example of risk analysis and risk treatment, situated in the context of the public/not-for-profit sector. Critically, this illustrates the setting of risk criteria and modelling of losses in non-financial terms.

Risk Criteria

Before embarking on the process of risk analysis and risk treatment, one must first revisit the discussion of risk criteria in Chapter 4. In that chapter, I looked at two risk criteria:

- How much are stakeholders willing to pay to reduce the probability of an extreme event? and
- How much are stakeholders willing to pay to reduce variability in outcomes?

With regard to the first criterion, I specifically looked at how much stakeholders are willing to pay to reduce the risk of bankruptcy. In this example, I am principally concerned with reducing the likelihood of a non-financial extreme event: failure to deliver a contracted (or statutory) service.

Let us consider the example of a not-for-profit organisation that has been commissioned to deliver a particular service to a specified number of people every year on behalf of a public body. Failure to deliver to the agreed number of people could impact on multiple stakeholder groups, including:

- People who may not receive the service that they were entitled to when they were expecting it;
- Staff members who may lose their jobs because the likelihood of winning similar contracts in the future is reduced; and
- Senior management who may suffer damage to their reputation.

It may be possible to estimate a financial cost of these outcomes and, from this, calculate the value of incrementally reducing the likelihood of failure (as I illustrated in Chapter 4). However, as I will show below, this is not strictly necessary in this example to demonstrate the benefit of a specific risk treatment.

Risk Analysis

In this example, delivery of this service is critically reliant on a particular piece of equipment, which operates 24/7, except for planned maintenance. Absent any unplanned downtime, the equipment has the capacity to provide a service to 1,000 people in a year. However, if the equipment experiences any downtime during the year, there is no way of making up for this, so the total number of people to whom the service can be delivered in that year is reduced, potentially falling below the contracted level.

It has been observed (or estimated) that the equipment experiences an average of five periods of downtime per year. A distribution of the duration of downtime has also been constructed, and this has then been converted into a distribution of the loss of capacity from disruptions. This might look something like the graph shown in Figure C.1.

One proceeds, as before, to combine the frequency and likelihood distributions using a Monte-Carlo simulation. This yields the following distribution of the loss of capacity over a year (Figure C.2).

Summary statistics of the distribution are as follows:

■ Expected loss of capacity = 21.4 people;
■ Standard deviation of loss of capacity = 15.9 people; and
■ There is a 5% chance of a loss of capacity of 53 people or more.

For the sake of illustration, I will assume that there are no other significant risks to service delivery although, in reality,

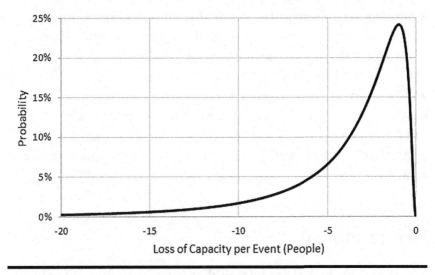

Figure C.1   Lognormal distribution of loss of capacity per event (expressed in terms of people)

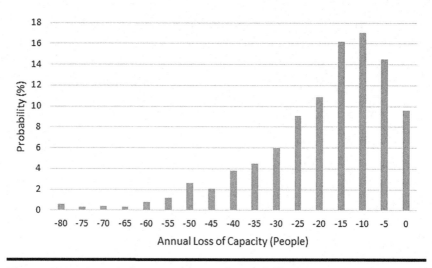

Figure C.2 Output from Monte-Carlo modelling (1,000 iterations) of annual loss of capacity

absence of staff and availability of other equipment/consumables would likely be other important constraints on capacity. Thus, with these simplifying assumptions, Figure C.2 represents the aggregated loss distribution for this analysis. Returning to the previous discussion on risk criteria, multiple stakeholders are keen to avoid a situation where the organisation cannot deliver to the number of people that it has been commissioned to provide to. In view of this, the organisation will presumably have allowed some sort of buffer: it will not have committed to delivering at the theoretical capacity of 1,000. If, for instance, the organisation has committed to delivering to 950 people every year, there is a 6.2% chance of not achieving this in any given year.

Risk Treatment

I now consider a risk reduction that caps the length of any downtime at the level at which capacity is reduced by 15

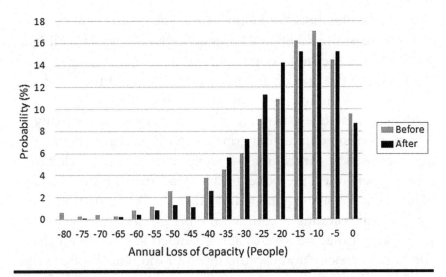

Figure C.3   Comparison of annual loss of capacity before and after risk treatment

people. This might involve a call-off contract to deliver replacement equipment within a specified period of time, or a plan to transfer work to alternative equipment located elsewhere within a specified time frame. The distribution of losses before and after the risk treatment is shown in Figure C.3.

Summary statistics of the before and after distributions show the effect:

■ Expected loss of capacity is reduced from 21.4 to 19.9 people;
■ Standard deviation of loss of capacity is reduced from 15.9 to 12.5 people; and
■ There is now a 5% chance of a loss of capacity of 43 people or more.

Critically, the annual likelihood of not delivering to 950 people has been reduced from 6.2% to 2.8%. Looking at this another way, the organisation could reduce its safety margin, and now commit to providing a service to 960 people each year, with only a 6.5% likelihood of failure. Thus, this risk treatment is worth at least the additional revenue derived from providing a service to another ten people each year.

Following the approach advocated throughout the book, one should be more precise about which particular stakeholder groups benefit from the risk treatment, but this really depends on the contractual arrangements. At one extreme, if the organisation can charge the same rate for these additional service users, then the benefits largely accrue to internal stakeholders (senior management and other staff). Alternatively, if the commissioning organisation has significant negotiating power, it may be able to agree a much lower rate for the additional capacity and capture much of the benefit of the risk treatment. Service users and/or tax payers may also benefit from either increased capacity or reduced cost of delivering the service.

Appendix D: Some Useful Sources of Risk Information

Information Security

BCI Cyber Resilience Reports https://www.thebci.org/knowledge/

Data Centre Incident Reporting Network (DCiRN) https://www.dcirn.org/

GDPR Enforcement Tracker https://www.enforcementtracker.com/?#

UK Department for Digital, Culture, Media and Sport, Cyber Security Breaches Surveys https://www.gov.uk/government/publications/

UK Information Commissioner's Office https://ico.org.uk/

US Department of Health and Human Services, Office for Civil Rights, Breach Portal https://ocrportal.hhs.gov/ocr/breach/breach_report.jsf;jsessionid=55DECB8D2E9DCAB29F50CE256C5D0439

Natural Disasters

CRESTA Industry Loss Index https://www.cresta.org/clix

EM-DAT, the International Disaster Database https://www.emdat.be/

The Natural Disasters (NATDIS) Database https://www.cat-nat.net/natdis-database

Desinventar Sendai https://www.desinventar.net/

Other

BCI Supply Chain Resilience Reports https://www.thebci.org/knowledge/

Blackout Simulator http://www.blackout-simulator.com/

Global Terrorism Database https://start.umd.edu/gtd/

ORX Banking Operational Risk Loss Data Reports https://engage.orx.org/download/annual-operational-risk-loss-reports

Sedgwick Product Recall Reports (US and EMEA) https://www.sedgwick.com/news

Sigma Research Reports https://www.swissre.com/institute/research/sigma-research.html

Index

Printed in the United States
by Baker & Taylor Publisher Services